Learning in Mrs. Towne's House

A teacher, her students, and the woman who inspired them

Tzivia Gover

Printed and published by
Levellers Press
Amherst & Florence, Massachusetts

ISBN 978-0-615-40869-9

Grateful acknowledgment is made to the following for permission to reprint previously published material: W. W. Norton & Company: Lines from "Remember" from SHE HAD SOME HORSES by Joy Harjo, copyright © 2008 by Joy Harjo. Reprinted with permission.

Portions of this book originally appeared in slightly altered form in the following publications:

"Mrs. Elizabeth Towne: Pioneering Woman in Publishing and Politics," *Historical Journal of Massachusetts*, Institute for Massachusetts Studies, Westfield State College, Vol. 37 (1), Spring 2009

"The Story of Elizabeth Towne," *Hampshire Life Magazine, The Daily Hampshire Gazette,* October 31, 2003

"The Long Road to Commencement," *Hampshire Life Magazine, The Daily Hampshire Gazette,* June 24, 2004

For my mother, Jane Covell,
and for
Elizabeth Towne (1865–1960)

and all of the young women
who've come into her house to learn

"what to say
about silence

the pages
left
unwritten..."

                              "qué decir
                                  ante
                              el silencio

                              las páginas
                              que se quedan
                              sin escribir..."

from "The Other Side of Night" / "Del otro lado
de la noche," Francisco X. Alarcón

TABLE OF CONTENTS

ACKNOWLEDGMENTS

For research assistance I owe my gratitude to Devon Dawson, who helped me find Mrs. Towne even before I knew her name, and the staffs at Mount Holyoke College Archives and Smith College Library and Archives.

I am so fortunate to have come to know Elizabeth (Betsy) Bruning in the course of my research. I am grateful for our telephone conversations and correspondence about her grandmother, and for her kind and patient presence throughout the process of my research. I am also grateful to Tink and Richard Linhart and Garrison Twing for sharing their family stories with me. And of course, to Mrs. Towne, for bringing us all together.

For helping to shape this story into words I thank Debra Scherban of *The Daily Hampshire Gazette* and Charlotte Meryman, Marty Dobrow, David Maloof, and Lori Soderlind. And 11,000 thanks to Lesléa Vazquez Newman for her editing assistance, her feedback, and most of all, her fabulous gift of friendship. Thank you to Karen Levy, for helping me get the words right, and to David Kahn for his deep friendship and love—and for encouraging me to get this book into print.

Special thanks to Yari, Marissa, Arelis, Veronica, and Nilda for welcoming me into their homes and for sharing their life stories with me; to Monica for letting me use her words; and to Marta Montalvo for sharing her poems, her determination, and her wisdom.

For teaching me to teach, I thank Daniel Judah Sklar and Stephen O'Connor, who were my mentors at Teachers and Writers Collaborative. And many thanks to Rhonda Soto for her friendship and inspiration.

For their support of my work at The Care Center I owe a debt of gratitude to Anne Teschner and Ana Rodriguez and all of the students and staff who bring a spirit of creativity and integrity to the tasks of teaching and learning. And special thanks to Aimee Loiselle, Carmen Vicenty, Sury Solivan, and Lisa Meidlinger for letting me come into their classrooms to teach poetry in the years when the events in this book took place. Thank you to Ezra Parzybok for help with the cover photograph. Special thanks to Judith Roberts for introducing me to Mrs. Towne. I am also grateful for the kindness and gentle guidance of Selenia Vazquez; although she is no longer with us, I'm sure her spirit continues to bless the halls and classrooms of The Care Center.

I am ever grateful for my unique and loving family: Dick and Diane Gover, Jane Covell, Joanne Yoshida, and James Gover, and to my daughter, Miranda, for putting up with endless dinner table conversations about Mrs. Towne.

Cover design by Riva Danzig of Danzig Design Group.

AUTHOR'S NOTE

"Life is very nice, but it lacks form. It's the aim of art to give it some."
—*Jean Anouilh, French dramatist*

The process of taking a living, breathing story, which in this case bridges three centuries and is peopled by hundreds of characters, and arranging it neatly onto a few hundred sheets of paper—all while keeping it true to life—is a challenging act. In doing so, I relied on a combination of research, interviews, diaries, and, of course, that very fallible but necessary tool: memory.

The sections about the life of Elizabeth Towne are all based on accounts from newspapers, magazines, books, letters, and papers written by or about the subject, as well as conversations with Towne's living relatives. When scenes are reconstructed, the facts used are gleaned from these sources.

In writing the sections about my work at The Care Center, I relied on my journals, memories, and interviews with past and current students and staff members. However, because many of my students were minors at the time the events in this book took place, and to honor the privacy of students whose permission I was unable to obtain, I have changed names and identifying details in most cases. I have used composite characters to simplify an otherwise overly complex or potentially confusing storyline. Because of this, the student authors credited with writing the poems included herein should not be assumed to be the work of any particular character described in the book.

I have listed in the endnotes specific sources from which information was gathered where possible and as appropriate.

CHAPTER ONE

THE INTERSECTION OF
CABOT AND OAK

THE FIRST TIME I APPROACHED WHAT I WOULD SOON COME TO REGARD as Mrs. Towne's house, I turned off the highway at Exit 16 and drove from intersection to intersection along Beech Street, feeling as if I were moving down a gangplank. I had been working as an editor at the county newspaper in nearby Northampton, Massachusetts, an upscale college town, when I decided to volunteer at The Care Center, where I would teach teenage mothers to write. I was ready, I had decided, to put my ideals about education and civic responsibility into practice.

Drivers who enter Holyoke from the interstate are greeted by a sign that boasts that the city is the "Birthplace of Volleyball." Chamber of Commerce staff will tell visitors that Holyoke was the country's first planned industrial city. But, located just north of Springfield in the western part of the state, Holyoke has many other claims to fame as well—not all of which the Chamber of Commerce would like to see emblazoned on a sign at its gateway. The city became known as the arson capitol of the region, after a spate of suspicious fires in the 1970s gutted tenement after tenement. When I first came to know the city in 2000 I learned that it has among the highest car insurance rates in the area due to the prevalence of car theft and uninsured drivers. Holyoke also has the distinction of having the first or second highest rate of teen pregnancy in the state, depending on the year. It also has a disproportionately high number of adults (one in three) who lack a high school diploma, and as a bookend to that statistic, a high incidence of poverty (one in four families).

Nestled between the affluent communities of South Hadley, home to Mount Holyoke College, and Northampton, home to Smith College, Holyoke has the air of a neglected stepchild. The downtown streets, which as recently as the 1960s teemed with shoppers and people out for an early evening stroll, are now all but deserted after five o'clock on most weeknights. Shop windows are covered with soapy swirls and faded placards announcing that they are for rent, lease, or sale. An article in *The New Yorker* magazine described Holyoke, with its downtown canals that run east to west, bisecting rows of aging factory buildings, as "a dilapidated Venice." These waterways, dug by hand by newly arrived immigrants at the turn of the twentieth century, powered the mills that once crowned the city with glory.

As I drove the city's streets that March, on nearly every storefront and lamppost I saw posters bearing the photograph of police officer John D. DiNapoli, who had been killed just before Christmas in a downtown shootout. Souped-up Toyotas thundered past bearing messages written in the same white paste I associate with the words *Just Married* on the backs of newlyweds' cars. Except in this case the words read "RIP Wilito," or "RIP Christian," creating moving memorials to young men killed in gang violence on those streets.

That year's census would tally the city's population, which had at one time exceeded 60,000, at just shy of 40,000. The demographics were not merely shifting; they were churning. In twenty years, 16,000 white residents had left Holyoke, while the Hispanic population had grown by more than 10,000—an astounding 170 percent. By 2000, just under half the city's residents were Hispanic, mostly from Puerto Rico. The young women I was on my way to meet that day were among the city's newest residents. They had moved north from Ponce, Bayamón, or San Juan, Puerto Rico—some by way of Brooklyn or the Bronx.

As I drove deeper into the city, my white liberal rhetoric slipped out of my head, and all I could think of was whether I had theft insurance on my car and whether I still had the key to my steering wheel locking device—which I never bothered to use in Northampton.

I was surprised to find then that The Care Center was in what realtors might call a "leafy suburban neighborhood." The house at 247 Cabot Street spreads, somewhat imperiously, across a corner lot. It is on a street of large one- and two-family homes in various states of disrepair, with deep front porches, overgrown gardens, and peeling paint. A white sign on the narrow front lawn boasted the center's name in bold, purple letters. A totem pole–like structure on the other side of the walkway proclaimed, in its own way, that what took place here was out of the ordinary. The sculpture, an art project from a previous summer, was decorated with cement casts of students' faces, hands, and arms. A cast of a student's pregnant belly had been made into a planter filled with soil from which green vines would protrude in springtime.

I parked my car and walked past the clutter of strollers and infant car seats on the porch. A small calico cat sidled up to my ankles as I pushed the door open, and darted past me into the foyer.

"Don't worry, he thinks he lives here," said the receptionist, who was seated behind a glass partition. She told me she'd let the director of education know I had arrived, and motioned for me to sit and wait.

I sat among a handful of students who were seated outside the office, waiting until it was time to go to class. Looking around, I felt overdressed in my white turtleneck and brown and white herringbone trousers. It wasn't only that I was dressed too formally, but that I suddenly seemed to be wearing too many clothes. The students, who were sipping from cartons of orange juice and picking at muffins and bagels supplied by the center, wore shirts with cutaway shoulders and plunging necklines. Their post-pregnancy, stretch-marked bellies peeked out through the space left uncovered between shirt hems and the waistbands of their jeans. I smiled too hard and said hello, and they nodded in return.

I had decided to become a literacy volunteer that winter after seeing the movie *Hurricane*, which stars Denzel Washington as Rubin (Hurricane) Carter, who in the 1960s was convicted of killing three white men. I cried watching the movie, even though not many movies make me tear up. Racism was hardly a new concept for me, but the movie made me want to do more about it than complain to my white liberal friends. After seeing it, I began listening to cassette tapes of Martin Luther King Jr.'s speeches as I commuted to and from work. Books by and about Gandhi, Thoreau, and Raushenbush began to pile up on my bedside table. A teacher I'd once had used to say that you find your work where your talents and the world's need intersect. I loved to read and write, and I was opposed to injustice. Teaching people who weren't being well served by the system seemed like the direction I should pursue.

That spring, New York City was trying to counteract a teacher shortage in inner-city schools by offering classroom positions to non-teachers, in a sort of domestic Peace Corps initiative. I was seriously entertaining the idea of packing up my life and heading to New York when a friend suggested I could take a much less drastic step and teach in nearby Holyoke instead. So I called a literacy program that was a short drive from where I worked, and made an appointment to find out more about becoming a volunteer.

The volunteer coordinator, a young, white woman wearing a loose-fitting jumper that bulged at the abdomen, appeared to be about seven months pregnant. She described about a half dozen agencies in the city that needed volunteers: one was for migrant workers, another for men and women who were studying grade-school-level reading and math, another combined literacy and job training, and so on. When she described The Care Center I decided I wanted nothing to do with it. Teaching teenagers would be challenging enough, but I didn't want to be in a place where motherhood was the central theme.

"I usually ask people where they'd like to volunteer, but I have a feeling that you'd be just perfect for The Care Center," she said. It was as if she could read my mind—only backwards.

"To tell you the truth, I'm not so sure about that," I said. I had my reasons, but I hoped I wouldn't have to get into any of that just then.

She took a moment, during which I thought perhaps she'd compromise and send me to teach the migrant farmworkers. Then she shook her head. "I think you'd be perfect there, and they really need a volunteer right now."

I reminded myself that I had intended to go where the need was strongest. I wrote down the address and phone number of the center and told her I'd call that week.

I had been waiting in the foyer for nearly ten minutes. The girls who'd been sitting near me had dispersed and gone to their classes. It was quiet now, except for the sound of a baby crying in the day care room. I had begun to examine the visual cacophony of student art projects, inspiring quotations, and magazine articles about parenting, which had been tacked to the walls of the hallway, when finally, Ana, the center's director of education, emerged from the stairwell. She exchanged a few words in Spanish with the receptionist, then, switching to English, asked me to follow her upstairs.

The door to Ana's office was decorated with a poster of a white wolf and a mobile made of wood and feathers. Inside, she took a seat at her desk, and I sat in the chair opposite. She explained that the center enrolled about sixty students at a time, but because students were constantly leaving and returning due to maternity leaves or a wide variety of other reasons, the school served more than a hundred students a year. These students, who'd dropped out of school, were all either pregnant or parenting. Although the school's mission was to serve those who had reading and math skills at the level of sixth grade or higher, Ana admitted that some of the girls were reading at the second or third grade level. They were divided into four classrooms, according to academic level and English language abilities. Because some had just come from Puerto Rico, two of the classes were conducted primarily in Spanish. Despite the students' various academic challenges, they all shared the same goal: to get their GED. Ana's words swirled by me as I tried to sort out the mixture of anticipation and fear that was pulsing inside me as I contemplated becoming part of the colorful chaos of the center. When she was finished with her introduction, Ana asked me to tell her about myself.

"I'd like to try teaching poetry during my volunteer time," I told her. During graduate school, I explained, I'd taught poetry in an inner-city school in New York, and I was eager to try the same techniques at the center.

"That's good," Ana said. Her dark hair was cut into bangs and she wore a ponytail pulled high on her head. Her hands rested on the desk in the pose of an administrator, palms facing inward, fingertips lightly touching. But her nails, which were intricately painted with turquoise polish accented by silver spirals and dots, were decidedly *not* those of a typical administrator. I couldn't take my eyes off them. "I think you'll work very well with Judith," she said. Judith, she explained, taught the higher level students who were studying in English. "Just tell her what you're interested in."

After another few minutes of ironing out details—which day I'd begin, what time I'd arrive, and so on—I took a deep breath. "I have one more question."

Ana tapped her fingernails smartly against each other and trained her lively brown eyes on me.

"I'm a lesbian, and I wondered if that's something I should mention to my students at some point. I wouldn't bring it up necessarily, but if they ask me whether I'm married, do you think I should tell them the truth?"

Ana's lips tightened into a frown, then burst open in a surprised laugh. This was new for me. Although I'd been out for more than a decade, I rarely announced my sexual orientation so directly. Usually, when I met new people, I just mentioned my partner and used the feminine pronoun. But I knew that here most of my students would be Hispanic and either Catholic or Pentecostal, and I thought sex roles would be strictly defined in this culture. Also, I'd been told by the volunteer coordinator that I should expect a lot of personal questions from my students. Secretly, I worried that the young women would have boyfriends who were members of gangs and who might want to beat up lesbians.

"I'm sorry," Ana coughed between gasps of laughter. "It's just you don't look like one." After she resumed her professional posture, she concluded: "I wouldn't go out of your way to bring it up, though."

I'm not sure how we closed that conversation, only that in spite of it, a few days later I returned to observe Judith's class in preparation for taking it over for an hour each week.

I sat in a chair with an attached desk along with twelve young women, while Judith, a small woman with pale skin, freckles, and bouncy red hair, stood in front of the class. Maria sat in the back row, slumped into her seat, her razor-straight, black hair curtaining her face as she read out loud from the page in front of her: "Having left high school at fourteen to marry her first husband, by 1898 Elizabeth Lois Struble Towne..."

Although no one but Maria was speaking, the room wasn't quiet. It was as if the hum of thoughts inside the students' minds—thoughts of what they would do when they got out of this place that day or for good—were somehow audible in the form of a restless buzzing. Or maybe it was just the indifferent hum of the space heater, crouching in the front corner of the room.

Outside, the sidewalks were still crusted with snow, but despite the weather Maria was dressed in a short-sleeve T-shirt that didn't cover the skin between the waistband of her pre-faded jeans and her navel. None of the students wore long sleeves or sweaters. I wondered if this was an issue of fashion or necessity. Probably, one had been born of the other, I thought.

"Keep reading," Judith prompted.

Maria flicked her hair out of her face, then finger-combed it back to exactly where it had been. "Elizabeth Struble Towne was thirty-three and faced her life—two children, a dull marriage and a household income that barely made ends meet—with the grim cheerfulness of her Oregon pioneer forebears. Then a spirit spoke to her."

"Excellent." Judith's praise was meant both as encouragement for Maria to continue and as sincere enthusiasm for her progress. Maria, who was twenty-one and a single mother, was just months away from "aging out" of the center. She had dropped out of the ninth grade to work, got pregnant soon after, and was now studying for her GED while her sister looked after her five-year-old daughter. I wondered whether she noticed the similarities between herself and the subject of the article she was reading.

For this day's history lesson, Judith had made a dozen photocopies of the article "Positive Thinking: New Thought Blossomed in Holyoke," which had appeared four years before in the local newspaper. Judith designed this unit on Holyoke's history to help her students better understand their city. Now, as she praised Maria and encouraged her to continue, I noticed that Judith, dressed in pressed jeans and a simple blue blouse, didn't look much older than her students, although she was in her forties, more than twice their age.

Her exuberance, which seemed natural to her, also seemed like a necessary trait in a setting like this. Maria and her classmates were battling hopelessness every day. Some were there reluctantly; they needed to fulfill a welfare requirement that mandated they be employed or enrolled in an educational program in order to receive benefits. Others had chosen to come, but still, they were frequently absent, and when they were present, they would fall asleep at their desks, or feign indifference to the lessons their teachers had prepared, rather than admit to their fear of failure. Ana had warned me of all of this, and I could see that it would take the persistent optimism of teachers like Judith to outpace the despair that seemed a more logical response to everything these students faced outside of these walls.

Maria continued to read: "Towne gathered her two children and left O-re- how do you say that?"

"Oregon," Judith said. She pointed to the state on a map in front of the classroom. "It's w-a-a-y out here." She made the word last as she dragged her index finger across from the western edge of Massachusetts, approximating the area where the school was located, then toward the Pacific Ocean.

Judith seemed unfazed by the fact that this paragraph was taking nearly an entire minute to read. The words, as they came out of Maria's mouth, were pulled apart syllable by syllable. The next reader, Sylvie, a young woman whose eyes were ringed with heavy black liner, continued only slightly less laboriously. Meanwhile, the list of unknown or unpronounceable words continued to grow. *Grim. Pioneer. Forebears. Oregon.*

I followed along with the students, staring down at the article in an attempt to model good attention skills. I kept my focus on the page in front of me, instead of looking out the window over the shingled rooftops to the Holyoke mountain range in the distance, as was the young woman to my left. Nor was I completing a find-a-word puzzle under my paper, like someone in front of me was now doing. Gradually, in fact, I was becoming interested in the story we were reading.

As the students strung together the words and sentences before them, details of Elizabeth Towne's life began to emerge. Although she never finished high school, had two children before she reached her eighteenth birthday, and faced poverty, Towne went on to publish *Nautilus*, a magazine with an international circulation. After divorcing her first husband, and remarrying, she also became a leader of the New Thought movement, a precursor to the New Age movement, whose followers focused on spiritual healing and positive thinking. Towne was also the city's first woman to hold elected office (as alderman at-large), the city's first female mayoral candidate, and a suffragist.[1]

By now, I was reading ahead on my own, no longer paying attention to Judith or the halting efforts of the student who was taking her turn plowing through another sentence. To me, Elizabeth Towne had suddenly surpassed everyone else in the room as the most interesting character present.

Sitting among these teen girls, I couldn't help but remember the pain of being that age myself. I remembered the struggle between the independent spirit blazing inside me and the silent but all-pervasive message from my peers, my parents, and even the sitcoms I watched, that the ultimate goal was to fit in: Be a lady. Be quiet. Be small. I would have liked to have known a woman like Mrs. Towne back then, a woman who could show me how to be strong and self-reliant. And here in this classroom, where I felt myself like a ghost, with my white skin and the transparency of not belonging, I would like to have a woman like Mrs. Towne to guide me. Everything I was reading made me think she and I would get along well. She was a publisher, she was a feminist, she was drawn to new ideas about healthy eating and spiritual wellness—all interests I shared.

I broke from my determined reading, however, when Judith directed the class's attention to the photograph that accompanied the article. It showed a sprawling structure made of red-pressed brick and limestone with dark wooden shingles beneath a gambrel roof. The building was marked by a jumble of dormers, windows, and porches, and looked as if it couldn't make up its mind whether to appear official or homey.

"That's The Care Center!" Maria said.

Of course, I thought, silently chiding myself for having missed the obvious.

Judith nodded. "Elizabeth Towne lived here, in this very house," she said.

It was decidedly uncool for the students to show interest in something the teacher was presenting, but I couldn't help but notice Sylvie's eyes shift from the page, which she had been covering with hearts and the names of her three-month-old baby and her boyfriend, to Judith's secondhand metal desk with drawers that stuck and stuttered when she tried to open them. I followed her gaze to the cream-colored walls marked by squares of old Scotch tape and smudges of ink and then to the solid oak door, built-in bookcases, and window trim. "So what was this, her bedroom or something?" Sylvie asked.

"You think the lunchroom was her kitchen?" another girl wondered aloud.

"Maybe she died here," someone else said.

Judith, I noticed, looked quite pleased with herself. "Let's see if we can find any of the answers in the article," she suggested. "Latisha, why don't you try the next paragraph?"

Elizabeth Towne arrived in Holyoke on May 26, 1900, just months after divorcing Joseph Holt Struble, a railroad station manager and the father of her two children. She'd packed the workings of her fledgling magazine into a trunk, and crossed the country to marry a William E. Towne, whom she'd come to know after he had written to the editor of *Nautilus* magazine to inquire about advertising rates. The day the Townes moved into the house on Cabot Street, the magnolia tree in the yard burst into flower—as if in welcome.

Neighbors would come to refer to the house, where dandelions sprouted enthusiastically on the lawn, as "Mrs. O. B. Joyful's" place. A wisteria vine, roses, and the looming magnolia tree gave color to the lot—but back then, it was the lady of the house who supplied the vivid color that would long be remembered.

Elizabeth Towne, I would come to learn, was the type neighbors would push aside a curtain to keep an eye on. She was a divorcee known to preach positive thinking and rigorous deep breathing. The windows of her house were open in all seasons to accommodate her belief in the necessity of fresh air to maintaining one's health and happiness. Birds flew in and out of the upper stories while her husband William's cats lay sunning on the upstairs porches. In the years during which the Townes were experimenting with what was then the rather unusual idea of vegetarian dining, lunch at the house might consist of a handful of nuts and a few pieces of fresh or dried fruit. And when Mr. and Mrs. Towne returned from their European travels, they would bring back what were considered by their Yankee neighbors to be exceedingly strange practices, such as serving cocktails before supper, and hanging large metal gongs in the dining room, which a housekeeper would beat to announce meals. For a time, Mrs. Towne even took up the unladylike habit of smoking cigarettes.

In the photograph that accompanied the article Judith presented, Towne had a head of wavy hair that was pinned up away from her face. She looked out at the future with a contented, open-lipped smile and eyes that sloped down at the outer corners. The Holyoke that Towne adopted as her new home was well matched to her natural optimism and desire for improvement and progress. Incorporated less than thirty years before, the city was, like Towne, just coming into its own. The population was growing steadily due to the immigration of workers from Ireland, Germany, and Canada, who flocked to Holyoke in search of jobs. These new immigrants filled the city's tenements, which had sprung up in neighborhoods surrounding the mills. As more and more laborers arrived, a construction boom ensued.

From the upper stories of her house, Towne could practically watch the city grow. She could see the smokestacks from newly built factories rise in the distance, just beyond the clock tower marking the great stone edifice of City Hall. Looking farther into the distance, she could make out the soft curves of the mountains that shaped the horizon.

The next Tuesday, a chilly early spring morning, I arrived at the center just as the silver van, which transports students from their homes to the school, was pulling up to the curb. Young women in short jackets or hooded sweatshirts climbed out one at a time, then turned to lift their babies. I noticed that the students who remained on board helped unbuckle the car seats and pass the infants forward and into the mothers' waiting arms.

The girls filed into the center, then turned left into the day care where they settled their children, before coming into the lunchroom where cold cereal and small cartons of milk were waiting. I continued to the right, and went down the hall to the photocopy machine, where I made copies of the poem I had decided to use for our first lesson.

I had been surprised that Ana agreed so easily to let me use my volunteer time to teach poetry. After all, anyone could plainly see that these students had more immediate and concrete needs. In order to pass the GED, their first step toward college or a better than minimum-wage job that could support them and their children, they would have to learn basic math skills, geometry, and algebra; learn how to answer questions about science and social studies; and write a persuasive five-paragraph essay. Even I had to admit that learning to identify stanzas and construct metaphors was not going to help them earn the money they needed to buy Pampers, pay the electric bill, or buy a car that could take them to a job or school. Nor would studying poetry put food on the table.

I climbed the stairs to Judith's second-floor classroom carrying my Virginia Woolf tote bag, which was stuffed with copies of Joy Harjo's poem "Remember," my copy of the textbook *Poetic Forms* and a ream of loose-leaf paper. I organized my things on Judith's desk and reviewed my lesson plan. Then, eager to begin, I stood in front of the whiteboard, marker in hand, as the students filed into the room. They shuffled past me, unsmiling, as if they were being herded into a prison cell. They took their seats and leafed through coupon inserts from the local paper, searched their purses for strawberry- or lemon-scented hand creams, or scribbled notes to friends and boyfriends. I plunged ahead with my lesson anyway.

"What is poetry?" I asked the class. No one stopped what she was doing. No one looked up. Maria still sat in the back row, staring in the general direction of my knees. "I'm tired," another girl whined.

Latisha, a girl with red streaks in her black hair, raised her heavily mascara-ed eyes slowly, as if she were using them to lift a dictionary. "It has to rhyme," she said. She folded her arms over her chest and rolled her eyes skyward. "Now are we done?"

I ignored the question, corrected the assumption about rhyme, and directed the class's attention to the Harjo poem:

> Remember the sky that you were born under,
> know each of the star's stories.
> Remember the moon, know who she is...

"Where did this poem come from?" I asked. No one answered. "The poet wrote it, of course," I prodded, "but where did she get the ideas she put into her poem?"

Silence. Maybe the question was too abstract, I thought, so by way of offering a hint, I tapped my forehead.

"Her brain?" Yari offered.

"That's right, what part of her brain?" I coaxed. I looked around the room. The silence gripped me and threatened to drag me under. The page I was holding began to flutter as my hand shook. Yari, sitting in the center of the second row was looking up, expectantly. She was the only one in the room, I realized, who appeared to be the least bit interested in what I was saying. I met her gaze and raised my eyebrows, silently begging her to respond. But she had no answer, either. Teach *her*, I told myself. Forget the rest of the class and just teach her.

"Her imagination," I said, putting the paper down on the desk. Abandoning the Socratic approach, I kept talking. I explained that poems are a combination of memory and imagination, that we can look inside our hearts and minds to find ideas and the inspiration to write. By the time I passed out sheets of lined paper and suggested the students create poems about things they remember, I was acting purely on faith, the blind hope that maybe one student besides Yari had heard anything I'd said. I was operating on the illogical belief that because I was about to ask them to write, the students would pick up pencils and begin to craft sentences on the page.

Minutes slinked by. Maria got up and sharpened her pencil. Evelyn asked me to explain again what I wanted them to do. Then, miraculously, one by one they began to write. Slowly. Eking out their thoughts word by word:

I remember living in the projects.
I remember my mother saying *bendición* as I walked out the door.
I remember the day I had my son.
I remember feeling lonely.

Memory and imagination. I conjured an image of Elizabeth Towne sweeping into the same classroom, skirts trailing. I saw her at the whiteboard, marker in hand. She would write something confident and positive: "The only true happiness comes from a living interest in one's work; the only success from the expression of one's own individuality in his work."

At home that evening, I sat at the kitchen counter and pulled the girls' poems from my tote bag. Their handwriting was cramped, angular, stiffly embossed on the page; or penciled airily, hardly willing to settle on the paper; or with elaborate loops and swirls that seemed to want to hide the misspelled words and gawky grammar. They *had* written, after all, I thought. An odd mixture of elation and determination settled over me. I fell asleep that night planning my next lesson, plotting the right words to say to make them understand. There was no longer a question—I knew I'd be back.

A few weeks later I introduced the students to haiku. I explained that traditionally, a haiku is a three-line poem consisting of seventeen syllables. But instead of focusing on the specifics of the form, we concentrated that day on content. I explained that haiku should capture a moment filled with contradiction or mystery. The fact that these poems needed to be only three lines long was attractive to the girls, and they bent their heads over their papers in effort.

When it was time to read the poems out loud, Sylvie raised her hand first:

> The greatest love I've ever known
> My pregnancy broke us apart
> I have a memory forever.[2]

I was encouraged. Hand after hand shot up. Several more students read short poems about their babies and about their boyfriends. Evelyn had written:

> Big eye just staring at me.
> Beautiful baby.
> Loving me.[3]

Finally I looked at the clock and saw we only had five minutes left. "One more," I said.

"Teacher, I'd like to read a poem I've been writing at home. I started it after the first class. The 'I Remember' class."

If any of these students was going to start writing poetry at home, I wasn't surprised that it would be Yari.

Unlike many of her classmates, Yari didn't bother with makeup. Still, her dark eyes called attention to themselves—they looked sad and unguarded. She pulled her heavy black hair into a simple ponytail most days and wore her jeans and T-shirts tight—but that seemed more because of weight gain from pregnancy than any desire to show off her figure.

Yari had quit school at fifteen when she was four months pregnant. She had tried a couple of other GED programs, but she had dropped out because she wasn't making any progress. Still, she was determined. She wanted to prove wrong a neighborhood police officer who'd once told her, "You're going to end up in jail like the rest of your family." One of her brothers had done time for stabbing someone. "He's just bad," she had once said to me. Her oldest brother, who she always thought was the smartest and would be the first in the family to graduate from high school, gave up in his junior year, and has never been able to hold a job.

Despite everything, Yari was one of the few students who, when I asked the class to share what they had written, could be counted on to read her poems. But while her compositions sounded good enough, when I looked at the page I saw she had misspelled words as common as "hit," "where," and "nice."

Now, she unfolded a piece of paper that was tucked inside her notebook. She smoothed it against the desk, then said, "It's about my memories."

I looked at the clock. Judith would want to start the math lesson in four minutes.

"Let's hear it," I said.

"I want you to tell me if it's good," Yari said. I nodded, beginning to feel impatient. Finally, she began:

"It's called 'My Life.' It goes—" Yari squinted hard at the words on the page, as if they required great effort to make out:

> Since I was born I live so scared of what could happen to my mother and to us. Every morning I would think of where I was going to hide that night, why father, why mother? Now I was five. Please dad, promise not to drink.

She looked up, as if for permission to continue. I nodded.

> Now I was older and I thought things were going to be better, but now it came to something else. What is going on? Drugs are taking them away. I'm twelve years old and all alone, no one there. Why me? I'm just a little girl that wants to live.

> By the age of thirteen things just got worse. Empty house. Hardly any food. Hardly any furniture. It got so bad my father had promised me not to hit my mother ever again, but it happened one more time. Now my mother is gone, don't know where she is, and my father is stuck in the same place.

She kept her eyes fixed on the page as she made her way, word by word:

> One whole year without seeing my mother. My period came down. She wasn't there. I was so scared. Is she dead? Is she ok? Christmas day came. She called. Thank you, God. Now she's back.

Fourteen years old. My mom's back but the drugs are still there and my father is now in jail. Me, so ignorant, I made a mistake. Opened my legs, now I lost what was so special to me. Guy took advantage. His mother threw me out on the street. One whole week sleeping on the street. Nowhere to go.

Age fifteen. My family got back together, and I got pregnant. I'm so scared. A beautiful son I got.

Her breath caught in her throat and she began to cry as she read the final lines. Not knowing what else to do, I started to walk toward her, to put a hand on her shoulder, to comfort her in some way—but she raised her fingers slightly from the page, a gentle signal for me to stay where I was. She took a determined breath and finished:

Now I'm nineteen. Things are better with my parents. No more drugs. No more beatings. No more pain. Now I got two boys and I live on my own. Now I finally feel at peace, finally I can teach my two boys not to abuse and I will not use drugs. Even though I went through all of this it wasn't my parents' fault. This is what happens when drugs are involved. I love you mom. I love you dad. For being the best I have. Thank you God, for the family you gave me.[4]

When she was done, I pulled a packet of tissues from my purse and passed them across the room to her, but as each young woman took the packet to pass it along, she first grabbed a tissue for herself.

"Yari, look up," I said. "I want you to see that you're not crying alone." She lifted her head and glanced around the room to see her classmates dabbing their eyes and noses. "Now, you tell me whether your poem was any good."

"I guess it was okay," she said, a smile nudging its way onto her face.

"I guess it was," I agreed.

Week after week I came to The Care Center to teach my one-hour poetry class. Then, just as I was beginning to feel comfortable with my routine, Judith told me she'd be leaving to pursue an advanced degree at a university in Boston and a new teacher would soon take her place. Change, it soon became clear, would be the only constant at the center. Teachers came and went; classrooms were moved to meet new needs; and students appeared, disappeared, and reappeared again: they took maternity leave, were put on suspension for missing too many classes or for breaking school rules; they gave up, decided to try again, gave in to family pressure to find a job, lost their job, and came back. Government policies that affected welfare were also constantly shifting and the program was forced to make changes in response, because nearly all of the students received benefits.

The new teacher was Lisa. She was as vivacious as Judith and just as welcoming of me and my poetry lessons. Lisa had dark hair, white skin, and eyes that always looked surprised. She loved animals, and sometimes while I was teaching she would interrupt a lesson to announce that we had a visitor. She'd walk to the window and nudge it open several inches until a small grey or black or calico cat, whose nose had been pressed to the glass, could flatten herself against the sill and push inside. The students welcomed the disruptions while I did my best to keep their attention. Once, I suggested they write poems about pets or animals, which resulted in sad tales of puppies and kittens my students had let into their lives, become attached to, and then lost to untimely deaths or landlords who threatened eviction if they weren't removed, or that they had to leave behind when they moved into homeless shelters.

Sometimes while I taught, Lisa would leave the classroom to catch up on other work. One day, after I'd been volunteering for a few months, I had the class to myself. We had just read a poem by Lorna Dee Cervantes in which the narrator hinted at having had an abortion. The class erupted into an argument about whether a woman who "killed her baby" could be forgiven.

"I don't know what kind of a female could murder her own flesh," one girl hissed.

"Let's get back to the poem," I said, trying to get the class under control.

A couple of weeks later I brought in "Sestina," by Elizabeth Bishop, about a grandmother and child in a kitchen on a rainy day. First I told the students how a sestina worked: it is a thirty-nine-line poem in which six end words are alternated throughout the poem in a set pattern. I suggested we try to write one as a group.

Together, the girls agreed on six words, which we'd use as our repeating end words. As they called out their ideas I wrote each one on the board: flower, friend, chair, yellow, love, and phone. When I turned to face the class, Ivy raised her hand. "Teacher, you have a smudge," she said. She pointed to my nose and dug through her purse for a compact and a tissue. I took the mirror and saw that I had managed to wipe my ink-stained hand across the side of my nose.

Ivy was always intervening when anyone had an item of clothing or a wisp of hair out of place. I'd seen her raise her hand during one of Lisa's lessons to tell her teacher that her shirt had come untucked, or that a tag was sticking out from under her collar. Ivy was herself always perfectly put together. Her makeup was tastefully applied, her hair slicked and styled. Her sneakers matched her shirt, and everything she wore looked newly pressed or newly bought.

I thanked Ivy and handed her the dry-erase marker. "You take over for a minute," I said, and walked to the back of the room to swipe at the ink on my face.

The students were trying to figure out a line that would end in the word *flower*, while I stared into Ivy's small mirror and finished cleaning my face. Suddenly I heard Neri yelling something in Spanish. I understood the word *puta* and knew that whatever had just happened had already escalated into someone being called a whore. I spun around to face the class just as a chair crashed to the floor. Then Yari jumped up and slammed Neri across the face. Instantly, the rest of the students had formed a mass around the fighters. Swear words in two languages filled the room and all I could do was yell, "Please! Ladies!"

Just then two staff social workers burst into the room. One grabbed Yari, and one Neri. Miraculously, the room quieted and the rest of the students returned to their seats.

Lisa heard the commotion and rushed over to join the social workers. The three of them escorted the students into the office. With the drama now contained, I turned back to the class. "We could pause here and talk about what happened, or we could return to the poem," I said.

"The poem," Ivy said, and the others nodded.

I took my place at the board, and we continued to work. We'd composed three stanzas by the end of class, and I congratulated the girls on their ability to focus despite the trouble earlier.

Instead of rushing off when class ended, I waited for Lisa to return so we could discuss what had happened. I hoped she wouldn't tell me that I could no longer volunteer, given my inability to control the class. Instead, she listened as I recapped the incident in detail. We both agreed I was lucky that the social workers had been nearby when the fight broke out. "I guess I shouldn't have turned my back," I said.

Lisa laughed. "It wasn't your fault," she said. "Those two have it out for each other. It would have happened no matter who was teaching just now."

As I drove away that day, I realized how personally I'd taken the girls' fight. I was disappointed that I hadn't been able to stop them—but more than that, I was disappointed in my students.

And wasn't disappointment just what other people had expected me to find at The Care Center? When I told my friends I was teaching teen mothers in Holyoke, they inevitably asked me if I was scared—scared that my car might get stolen, that I might get mugged on my way to or from the center, that my students might have gang affiliations. I'd been looking forward to reporting back that their stereotypes—and my own—had been unfounded. My students had shown a genuine interest in poetry, I wanted to be able to say. We'd been reading Bishop, and in fact, they'd composed the first three stanzas of a sestina. But now I'd have this to report back: the girls in my poetry class—including Yari, the most promising, in my opinion—had lived up to the world's diminished expectations of them.

If You Can Touch This Poem[5]

If you can touch this poem
          You can touch me.
If you love this poem
          You will love me.
If you walk with this poem next to your heart
          You will fill your heart with my blood.
If you leave your memories behind when you read this poem,
          You'll live my memories.
If you go, keep walking and die
          With this poem on your side.
You will make my heart die with this poem.

CHAPTER TWO

FAMILY NOW

ON THE FIRST TUESDAY AFTER LABOR DAY I ARRIVED at The Care Center as if for the first time. I'd been volunteering there for two years—coming in a few minutes before class each Tuesday, hastily photocopying the poem I'd chosen to teach that day, and rushing off when I was done to return to my real job.

Students had come and gone in those years. Maria aged out of the center without ever getting her GED. Neri and Ivy graduated and had enrolled in the community college. Yari had gone on maternity leave and returned with another son, whom she'd recently begun bringing to the center's day care. Lisa had moved on and a new teacher, Aimee, had taken over her class.

I had moved on in a sense, too; I'd been hired as the staff writing instructor. Instead of one poetry class a week, I'd now be teaching four. I'd also teach an afternoon writing elective and would edit an annual anthology of student writing.

I had thought that the transition from being a volunteer to being on staff would have merely meant adding hours (and pay) to the time I had already been spending at the center, but that turned out not to be the case. Maybe what I was experiencing was similar to what friends described as the shift from a couple living together to being married. There's some intangible reordering of perspective that comes with a formal contract. As a volunteer, everything I did was more than was expected. Just by showing up I'd done a remarkable deed. Even the students had been impressed when one day their teacher said, "You know, Tzivia isn't paid to come here. She teaches you because she *wants* to." For a week or two after they learned this fact, which was to them incomprehensible, they were more attentive and better behaved during my class. Now that I was officially on staff I would perhaps become just another white woman who was in their lives because she was paid to be. For my part, I also had taken on the burden of feeling like I ought to belong. I was no longer that temporary, doted-upon entity known as "company." Now I was, as Ana would tell me, "family."

One of the perks of being on staff was that I would be given a home within the school: a desk, a shelf, a telephone extension, and a voice mailbox. It was Ana's job to find me an office, or as it were, a corner of someone else's office to share. We prowled the third floor, poking our heads into various rooms, including one that resembled a large closet and another that was already cluttered with too many desks. As we continued our search, Rhonda walked past, carrying an armful of boxes.

"Hey, Rhonda," Ana called out, "how about you sharing your new office with Tzivia?"

"No, that's okay," I interrupted. Rhonda was moving her things out of an office with two desks in it, and was headed down the hall to a recently vacated room. It was easy to see that she was moving from a two-person setup to a room of her own. "Don't answer now," I told Rhonda. "At least think about it."

"Of course I'll share with Tzivia," Rhonda said to Ana, as if I hadn't spoken. Ana and I followed her to the room at the top of the stairs. It was a small office under the eaves. A single window looked out over the trees to the rooftops of downtown Holyoke. The desk under the window would be mine, and Rhonda's would be the one closest to the door. I would soon come to appreciate the beauty of that arrangement, because nearly every visitor to our office that fall would be seeking Rhonda, not me. Ana thanked Rhonda and left us alone.

Rhonda had already begun hanging posters to cover the tired yellow walls. Her belongings were piled on a folding table that she'd dressed up with a lacy white tablecloth. Among her things were an electric fountain that sent a stream of water over a small pyramid of stones, framed pictures of her family, including a snapshot she'd enlarged of her father's dry-cleaning store in Harlem, a Puerto Rican flag, and a crystal ball that sat on a small metal tripod. "I don't know why I carry all this stuff around," she said as she emptied paperweights, bags of Chex mix, and books from a cardboard box.

While Rhonda drove nails into the walls to hang her bulletin board crammed with photos of students and their children, her framed certificates of appreciation from past jobs, and her marionette puppet in the shape of a furry green frog, I stuffed a few manila file folders into the bottom drawer of my new desk and Scotch-taped to the wall a series of index cards I'd printed on my computer, each bearing a quotation about poetry: "Poetry comes in the form of a blessing," Stanley Kunitz; "Poetry is telling my particular truth the way I see it," Gwendolyn Brooks; and "Poetry is free on every level," Lorna Dee Cervantes.

After years of living in New England and feeling too Jewish in a sea of Yanks, with Rhonda, I now felt I had found someone who was more ethnic than I was. Clearly, of the two of us, I would not be the loudest, most talkative, or most exotic (an adjective that has always made my skin crawl when used to describe me).

Rhonda taught athletics in the afternoons, so most days she dressed in sweats, sneakers, and a baseball cap. She was barely over five feet tall and her shoulder-length brown hair was usually pulled into a high ponytail that peeked out from under the band of her cap. She always seemed to be cracking jokes in her Bronx accent, high-fiving someone, then bending over laughing. She spoke to students as if she were one of them. Once, as I was passing by, I overheard Rhonda talking to a group of girls who were complaining about birth control. Condoms were "a pain," one said, and another added that she couldn't remember to take the pill. "I use the best birth control," Rhonda said, thrusting her chest and straightening her neck, poised for her own punch line.

"Yeah, so what is it?" Carmen asked.

"I don't have sex," Rhonda declared, and the girls burst out laughing. They exchanged high fives all around as I passed unnoticed on my way upstairs.

Now, Rhonda regaled me with stories of her life. Her mother was white and Irish, her father black and Puerto Rican. Her mom had left her father some fifteen years ago for a woman. Her father, meanwhile, had become a born-again Christian. Rhonda's mother, and all of her mother's siblings, married outside of their race, and when Rhonda's grandfather died, her Irish grandmother remarried a Chinese man who had been known to down a mugger with a casual sweep of his foot.

Growing up first in Harlem, then in the Bronx, Rhonda was a single mother who'd recently gotten off welfare. She had completed two years at the community college and was now enrolled part time at the elite Mount Holyoke College. She kept bags of candy on her desk for the students, who would come into the office at random intervals and help themselves. Taped to the wall next to her desk were little notes students had left her when they stopped by and found her absent: "I miss you, Rhonda," "I love you, Rhonda," and little happy faces that encouraged her to "keep smiling."

It took me less than a half hour to set up my corner of the room. When I was done, I helped Rhonda empty boxes and hammer nails. When it was time for me to go to my first class, she was still decorating.

I'd decided to start the semester off by having students write poems about their names. It would be a good way for me to get to know the new girls, I thought. Of course, I already knew many of them from previous classes. For example, Yari, who would soon be taking the GED for what she hoped would be the last time, was sitting in the first row, and then there was Sylvie, who had disappeared for more than a year (no one knew quite why) and had just as inexplicably returned, insisting she would stick it out this time. Latisha and Evelyn, who had both tried several times but hadn't yet passed the GED, were seated in the back.

"I don't wanna write no poem about my name," Esme, one of the new students, announced when I explained the assignment. "Why we gotta do that shit?" Although this was the first time I'd met Esme, I'd already been warned about her propensity for swearing.

"Who named you?" I asked.

"I have no fucking idea. My mother must have given me my name. I don't know."

I had been advised to be firm with Esme about using appropriate language in class, but I didn't want to start off with an argument, so I let it slide. "And why did she pick Esme? Why not call you Lucy, instead?"

"Lucy? Lucy's a white girl name. No one's going to be calling me no Lucy."

"When it was time to name your baby, did you think a lot about what you'd call him?" Esme nodded. "Well, don't you think your mother did the same thing when she had you? She thought about a lot of different names, and she picked Esme for you. Why was that?"

"I told you I have no idea. I just know my aunt is named Esme and my name is Esme, too."

"Well, then your mother must have chosen your name to honor your aunt. Who else?"

"I was named for my grandmother," Carmen said.

"I was named for a lady in a soap opera," someone else said.

"Think about what your name sounds like and what it makes you think about. If you don't like your name, think about what name would suit you better," I said as I handed out sheets of paper.

One girl I hadn't seen before was slumped into her chair. Her T-shirt was black with the word *Whatever* printed across the front in white. But the first thing I noticed about her was her size. She was squeezed between the chair back and the attached desk, making the piece of schoolroom furniture look as insignificant as a belt.

"What's your name?" I asked her.

"Ruth," she all but whispered.

Ruth's page was blank.

"How do you want to start?" I asked her.

She tightened her lips and shook her head from side to side.

"Who gave you your name?"

She shrugged her shoulders.

"Do you like it?"

Another shake of the head, more vigorous this time.

"Do you know the story in the Bible about Ruth?"

She raised her eyebrows.

"It's a story about friendship. It's a really nice story. You should read it. Ruth's a good name to have."

I picked up Ruth's pen. "Do you mind?" I asked.

She shrugged again.

"You don't like your name. Why?"

"My father gave it to me. It doesn't mean anything."

I wrote her words on the page. "What else?" I asked.

"I don't like it. I should read the Bible story."

Another student was calling for me. I finished writing what Ruth had said and slid the paper around to her. "You finish it," I said. "Fix up anything I wrote down wrong. Add anything that comes into your mind."

When class was almost over I handed out copies of Elizabeth Barrett Browning's sonnet, "How Do I Love Thee." "Next week we're going to read this poem together, but I want you to take a look at it first," I told the class.

"This poem is whack," Latisha said.

"And it's too long," Esme added.

"Well, how long is it? Count the lines." I explained that a sonnet has fourteen lines, and it has to rhyme. "Listen," I said, "see if you like it." As I spoke the poem aloud without referring to the paper, I could see the students' faces register the fact that I was reciting, not reading the poem:

> I love thee with the love I seemed to lose
> With my lost saints. I love thee with the breath,
> Smiles, tears, of all my life; and if God choose,
> I shall but love thee better after death.

The girls stared as if I had just produced a flea circus from my purse. One person began to clap. I turned around to see that it was Rhonda, standing in the doorway.

"That was great," she said.

"If anyone in this class can memorize it, I'm going to give her a prize," I told her.

"Yeah, she says that 'cuz she knows we can't do it," Latisha called out.

"Memorizing poetry *is* hard," Rhonda told the class, "but you should try it." The girls rolled their eyes and slumped deeper into their chairs. Latisha was resting her head on her arms, which were crossed on her desk. She cocked one eye up at Rhonda, and said, "Yeah, right."

"I've done it," Rhonda said.

I felt a glimmer of hope. If Rhonda, whom the girls thought was the embodiment of cool, recited a poem for them, maybe they'd give it a try.

"Go for it," I said, and took a seat at an empty desk near the door.

"I hope I remember it," Rhonda said. She turned her back to the class and took a couple of deep breaths. Then she spun around to face us and belted out a poem by Saul Williams, a hip-hop poet:

> if i could find the spot where truth echoes i would stand
> there and whisper memories of my children's future
> i would let their future dwell in my past
> so that i might live a brighter now ...

As the words flew from her mouth she began to move her hips, chest, and shoulders in rhythm with the poem.

> now is the essence of my domain and it contains
> all that was and will be
> and i am as i was and will be because i am and always will be
> that nigga
> i am that nigga
> i am that nigga ... [6]

When she was finished all I could hear was the silence of the girls' stopped breath. They were in awe. But not in awe as if she'd just completed a circus trick—in awe as if she had touched something inside them. After a moment they burst into applause and shouts of "You go, Rhonda," and "That was phat."

Back in our office that afternoon I sat at my desk reading students' poems, making corrections, and writing encouraging comments. Rhonda was gathering her papers into a shoulder bag and putting on her jacket. "I wish I could get through to them the way you do," I said.

"You have your own style. You give them something different."

I found myself quoting Ruth's shirt. "Whatever," I said.

"You take things too serious," Rhonda said. "Don't think about things so much."

—

Later that week, Ana called me into her office. "I know you've been around here for a while, but I want to formally welcome you onto the staff," she said. "Now you're part of the family." She moved toward me to shake my hand, I thought, but instead embraced me. I'm not the hugging type, so I was glad that the phone rang just then and she excused herself to answer it.

Observing Ana's nails had become a habit with me by now. Once a month she had them repainted in different tropical colors and meticulous designs. This day they were spring grass green with silver glitter flowers adorning each squared-off tip. As Ana listened to the caller at the other end of the phone, she clicked the nails of her right hand against the nails on the left, making a light tapping sound like rain on window glass. While she was talking I busied myself admiring the photographs on her bookshelf. The pictures were propped in front of books and between framed certificates of achievement, knickknacks, and trails of potted ivy that began on the top shelf and wound down and along the shelves.

Ana hung up the phone and pointed to the studio portrait of a young woman with cascading black hair. "That's my daughter," she said. "Do you recognize her? She was a student here." I shook my head. "She's in college now, studying to be a nurse," Ana said. She proceeded to identify the people in each photograph. She pointed out her other grown daughter, who still lived at home, and then her oldest, her son, who was born in Puerto Rico one month after Ana graduated from high school. Then she picked up the next frame, which held a snapshot of a little boy who was maybe three years old. "This is my grandson. He says he'll marry grandma someday," she said, her voice swelling with pride.

I took a step back and looked at Ana again. "You're a grandmother?" I asked. "You look too young!" I was being sincere. Her skin was caramel-colored and perfectly smooth. She was dressed in jeans and a brightly colored shirt with a bold design featuring fern leaves and pink flowers. Most days she wore sandals or sneakers and pulled her black hair into a perky ponytail.

"You're fishing for a raise already," Ana said, with a laugh tucked just behind her words. Then she studied me with frankness to equal my own. My brown hair was loose around my shoulders. I'd forgotten to put on earrings again and wore no makeup. "How old is your daughter?" she asked me.

I told her Miranda had just turned fourteen and was a freshman in high school.

"Then you can be a grandmother any time now, too," Ana said.

"God forbid!" I exclaimed. The response was automatic and, I thought, inevitable.

Ana blinked and pulled away, almost imperceptibly. What she did, I realized a moment too late, was wince.

For me the idea of my daughter becoming pregnant at fourteen, fifteen, or even twenty was horrific. First, she should finish high school, and then college, and if possible, gain an advanced degree or be well along on a career path. I'd like her to be married or at least in a long-term, serious relationship. A teenage pregnancy in our family would be treated as a crisis. We'd keep it private, telling only our closest friends. We'd likely go to family counseling to try to understand what had gone wrong.

Statistically, I knew it was likely that my daughter would have sex before graduating from high school. And if she did, she was prepared. In fact, she probably knew better how to handle premarital sex than she knew how to escape from a burning building. She knew that while I didn't approve of sex outside of a long-term, mature, and committed relationship, if she did sleep with a boy she should use a condom, make sure she was with someone she trusted, and never be afraid to come to me if there was a problem (a pregnancy) because we could take care of it (get an abortion before it was too late).

Ana had been that pregnant teenage daughter once. She was eight months pregnant at her high school graduation. She had also been the mother of a teen mother—hadn't she just finished telling me that one of her daughters had graduated from The Care Center? My reaction to Ana's casual observation that I could be a grandmother, too, told her that if I were in her shoes I'd consider myself a failure and my daughter a disappointment.

The sounds of parrots chirping in an Amazonian jungle interrupted my musings, as Ana's computer shifted into sleep mode and her tropical screensaver came to life.

Ana sat back at her desk. Our meeting turned back to business. We discussed the upcoming assembly, in which students would pick their elective classes, and Ana reminded me that I could always come to her if I had any questions or problems.

When we were done talking, I left and returned to my own office. I was leafing through books of poetry and trying to convince myself that my conversation with Ana hadn't been as awful as I thought it was, when Maria, the custodian, entered the room, wordlessly plunked her metal pail on the floor, and leaned her mop against the door. With hurried efficiency she pulled on a pair of latex gloves and began emptying the trash into a large plastic bag. I thought she looked like Carol Burnett; she was short, with dyed-red hair and round, expressive eyes. She said something to me in Spanish, but I shook my head. She repeated it, faster this time. Something about the impatience in her high voice made me nervous, and I couldn't remember even the rudimentary Spanish phrases I knew. She tied the trash bags off with a swift set of gestures and began to mutter, *"No entiende nada. No entiende nada."* She doesn't understand anything. She doesn't understand anything.

Even as I walked the two blocks to the city library, I couldn't have said exactly why I was going there. As a former journalist it was my instinct to *want* to understand. Perhaps the reason I had become a journalist in the first place was because the printed word had long been the best tool I knew to reach any satisfying degree of comprehension of the world around me. I had a vague notion then that I wanted to know more about the building The Care Center was housed in— that if I could understand the history of that small plot of ground, maybe I could also understand my place there in the present tense. I had a dim memory of the story of the suffragist and publisher who had once occupied those rooms and thought I'd start by looking for the article about her that Judith had handed out to the class on my first day at the school. But mostly, I think, the library represented a place I could escape into, where I could navigate through stacks and catalogs and databases with competency and ease.

The Holyoke Public Library stands at the center of a city block, surrounded by trimmed green lawns. But despite the abundant greenery and despite the words *Bienvienidos* and *Welcome* printed in bold black letters on the sign that lists the building's open hours in English and Spanish, the looming limestone edifice can seem to offer a chilly reception and the lawns somehow looked like a moat, intent on keeping danger at bay, rather than drawing visitors in.

Still, I love public libraries, almost as a matter of principle, and as I passed through the electronic gates and into the building I felt at home. Even as a child, in spite of what seemed the infinite complexity of life—the endless nuances of interaction in my family and at school, all of which I was helpless to interpret and understand—the library was a place where I could trill my fingers across cards lined stiffly in a catalog, or turn to the index page at the back of a book, and find a thread of information I could pick up, hold on to, pull gently, and begin to follow. And after I had collected my pile of cellophane-swathed volumes, I would be hypnotized by the prim efficiency of the librarian, as she thumped the due date stamp from the inkpad to the plate in the back of each book.

But this day, as soon as I entered the periodicals room, I realized I didn't have enough information to find the article I was looking for. I could have searched for the article by date, if I'd known it, or by the name of its subject, which I'd long since forgotten. The librarian suggested I try a search of the local newspaper's electronic archives using various keywords. But that was a dead end, too. I soon became discouraged, knowing I had too little information to go on that day—but I also felt a familiar tenacity taking hold of me. I'd be back, I thought, as I passed out through the electronic surveillance gates, this time empty-handed.

———

At the center I could do another kind of research. Every student was like a book to study. Every day there was a lesson for me to learn, a new question to ponder. Walking through the halls each day, I saw bellies like melons ripening in the sunshine, bellies like harvest moons rising above the waistbands of low-slung jeans. I saw stretch marks reaching from navels like branches of trees, like roads on an atlas. I regarded every round belly as a catastrophe. I knew for certain that teen pregnancy was wrong. A student who already had a toddler would come to class with one strap of her corduroy overalls unbuttoned and flapping down, her six-month pregnant belly cresting into view, and I wanted to send a condolence card. "How do you feel about it?" I'd ask. I expected tears, guilt, and shame. Usually she'd respond, "I just hope it's a girl this time," or "I'm glad he'll be born in the spring."

I expected teachers to treat pregnancies as a problem, too. They might even take them personally: if they were doing a better job, the girl wouldn't have gotten into this mess. But I couldn't help noticing the ways that motherhood was celebrated here. Classrooms had bulletin boards filled not only with student work (science projects, English papers, math worksheets) but also with pictures of newborns and toddlers. There were studio portraits from JC Penney with little boys standing in front of oversize cutouts of the number one or two on their first and second birthdays, or an infant lying in a bassinet under a backdrop of a window opened onto a starry sky, and even a baby girl swaddled in cotton, with silver wings strapped to her tiny shoulders and a halo perched above her head. One of the first things Rhonda had done when she set up her office, I now remembered, was to establish a collage of such pictures students had given her on a bulletin board behind her desk, so it would be the first thing students saw when they came in to visit her. When students walked through the halls balancing babies on their hips, the teachers cooed over them, exclaiming, "*que linda*," how beautiful.

During a special afternoon of art and poetry for the students called Phenomenal Women Day, one of the counselors led an icebreaker activity to get everyone out of school mode and into the mood to create and celebrate. We were seated at round tables as she called out questions. If the answer was yes, students were to stand up. She fired off her queries: If you have a brother, stand up. If you were born in New York, stand up. If you were born in Puerto Rico, stand up.

Students gave whoops of solidarity as they rose to their feet in answer to a question.

"How many have one child?" she asked. Nearly every student stood, leaving in their seats only a few who were expecting their first. "How many have two?" The girls raised their arms and cheered as they stood and smiled. "And three?" Sonia, who had just returned from maternity leave after giving birth to her third baby, got to her feet. The group let out a cheer. "Go, Sonia!" someone yelled. I sat in confused silence. The afternoon was beginning to feel like a pep rally for teen sex.

I'm not sure what I would have wanted instead. Would I rather have the staff treat students returning from maternity leave with quiet disapproval? Would I have liked to see more hand wringing, perhaps? If it were for me to decide, would I take down the pictures of smiling children that hung in classrooms and offices and replace them with fact sheets about problems associated with teen motherhood?

Students Beware: As teen mothers you face higher levels of STDs, are more likely to have children with physical, emotional, or learning disabilities, and are likely to attain lower educational levels and earn less money than older mothers. Your children are less likely to complete high school, and more likely to remain in poverty. And of course, your daughters are more likely to become teen mothers—just like you.

But of course the girls already knew all of this. Or at least, they were living it, and they had seen their mothers, aunts, cousins, and sisters live it, too. And in fairness to the center, the staff did do their part to help students make different choices.

In the second-floor bathroom at the center, there were two wicker baskets, each decorated with tulle ribbons wrapped around the handles. One contained trial-size bottles of shampoo and conditioner and small bars of soap. The other was filled with variously flavored and textured condoms. The contents of both were free for anyone who wanted them, and because they were discreetly located, girls could fill their pockets or pocketbooks in privacy. There were also posters hung at eye level, in English and Spanish, that read: "Oh no, the condom broke. What can I do?" The posters included information about the morning-after pill, an emergency contraceptive that could be effective for up to seventy-two hours after unprotected sex and which, the poster reminded, was available from the nurse on the second floor.

When a recent article in the local newspaper carried a report that Holyoke had dropped from having the first to second highest rate of teen pregnancies in the state, I heard some of the counselors say, with a smile, that they could take some credit for that shift downward. "We give out plenty of morning-after pills and we counsel them. We talk to them about birth control and other options," one counselor told me.

In Holyoke the latest census revealed that some 15 percent of the city's families were considered "female headed," meaning there was a single mother raising at least one child under age eighteen.[7] Just under half of children in the city were living in poverty.[8]

But the facts we rattled off at students stood in contrast to a cultural acceptance of, even encouragement for, large families and traditional roles of marriage and motherhood for young Latinas. Most of the young women came from religious backgrounds where abortions were looked on as cruel, blasphemous, or both. Many also came from rural areas where formal education was not nearly as useful as the ability and willingness to work in the fields or in the kitchen. Now they were living in neighborhoods where the welfare office was down the street and there was drug money to be made on every corner. Meanwhile, jobs were hard to come by. And even if a student managed to fill out the application correctly, find transportation to and from work (fewer than half the people in their neighborhoods owned cars), and arrange and somehow pay for childcare, their reward was likely to be a minimum-wage paycheck and no benefits.

The demographic these girls were born into—economically disadvantaged youth from single-parent homes—made teen motherhood seem almost inevitable.[9] Then there were the subtler, psychological disincentives to putting off motherhood. For these teens, motherhood was a known problem—financial success and independence were unknown. Having children young meant they would be embraced by their community—taking a different path meant loneliness and isolation.

I thought about Yari's mother, Marilu, who, at age ten, had married a young man who was seventeen. They were living in Michigan at the time, where a judge refused to marry the couple. In fact, he threatened to remove Marilu to state custody. "But I love her, what can I do?" her young suitor asked the judge. "I don't care what you do, but you can't do it around here," the judge answered. The couple then moved to Puerto Rico, where all they needed to be married were approving signatures from their parents. But Marilu soon learned that marriage wasn't the happy ending she'd dreamed of. Yari was Marilu's fourth baby and second daughter, and she hoped her youngest wouldn't follow her example. Yari's sister had gotten pregnant at sixteen, and before she was out of her twenties she had six children. But when at age fifteen, Yari told her mother she, too, was pregnant, Marilu was philosophical. She didn't believe in abortions, and so she adjusted herself to the news and began looking forward to being a grandmother again.

"I guess it's a family tradition," Yari said. Like rice and beans and pernil, or salsa and merengue, it was easy to paint teen pregnancy into the picture of Puerto Rican culture. Her mother's attitude toward a daughter who got pregnant before getting her high school diploma seemed a common one: frustration and anger, then acceptance and even celebration.

"How would your life have been different if you hadn't gotten pregnant?" Rhonda asked her students during a workshop that fall. I expected to hear the girls say that they'd have finished high school, enrolled in college, and been on the path to a good job. Or they might say they'd be free to go out with friends on a Friday night. They'd have time to do the things they wanted to do. Some said those things, but more said pregnancy had saved them. Those pregnant bellies worked like shields against drugs and living on the streets. They were tickets to free services, counseling, food vouchers, welfare—a second chance. And young mothers, the students explained, were less likely to get involved in the physical fights that plagued other girls in their neighborhoods.

Some studies confirm the idea that pregnancy is not always bad for young women. Unmarried pregnant teens are, according to at least one researcher, more likely to have high self-esteem, feel satisfied with their lives, and have positive feelings about their abilities than others their age.[10]

Each year when I compiled the students' poetry into an anthology, I asked the authors to compose short biographical statements. I suggested they include something they had accomplished that they were proud of, and a goal they hoped to achieve. Time after time, girls wrote that they were proud of their children, and their goal was to be the best mother they could be.

Yari was different, though. She talked about her dreams of being a police officer, then a correctional officer at the prison in nearby Ludlow.

She didn't get these ideas from her mother. Marilu's dreams for her youngest daughter were more traditional. "When she was little, I always pictured that one day she'd come out from the house in white and getting married like it's supposed to be … and having all the children she wants and being happy and doing whatever she wanted to do," Marilu would say.

The only concrete details in Marilu's vision for Yari were the white dress and the babies. The rest was amorphous, as if it were beyond her to conjure a clear image of any other options for her daughter's happiness.

I Am the Poet[11]

I am the poet of pregnancy, babies and children.

I am the poet of doing everything by myself.

I am the poet of the same bedtime stories every night. Over and over.

I am the poet of craziness.

I am the poet of being stressed out to the highest point that stress can get to.

I am the poet of never having time to myself. But why would I want to be alone?

I am the poet of blowing 20 million bubbles when we go outside to play.

I am the poet trying to think up things to get my son to brush his teeth when he doesn't want to.

I am the poet of throwing out all my makeup when my son decides to give himself tattoos with it.

I am the poet of lying with him until he falls asleep at night.

I am the poet of being a mother to my baby.

CHAPTER THREE

TIMELINES

IT WAS A WARM FALL MORNING, SO RATHER THAN DRIVE, I set out to walk the mile and a half from my house to work. I had moved to Holyoke that year, having fallen in love with the city despite—or because of—its struggles and contradictions. When I mentioned to my students that I was leaving Ashfield, a rural town an hour's drive up into the hills, to live instead in Holyoke, they were quick to express their disapproval. "Who'd want to live *here*?" Gloria asked.

To my students, Holyoke was a city of garbage and gangstas. But I had moved to the northern neighborhoods, where streets were named for colleges: Amherst, Princeton, Dartmouth, Radcliffe, Swarthmore, and Vassar. In this part of town, known as the Highlands, the trees were turning deep red and orange, and that morning leaves were dancing through the air, painting the day with shades of mustard and scarlet. Nearly all of the people in suits and overcoats climbing into their late-model Buicks, SUVs, and minivans were white. Technically, the street that led me from home to work was still Cabot, but this far north it was called River Terrace, and the rear windows and decks of houses on the north side of the avenue looked over the Connecticut River and out to the Holyoke mountain range.

In a sense, each day when I walked or drove down the hill to work I was following, in reverse, the migration of centuries of immigrants to the city. Historically, newcomers to Holyoke lived in a neighborhood known as the Flats, where streets lined with factories, brick row houses, and apartment buildings huddled between the canals downtown. Some of the tenements where the city's millworkers once lived now housed the unemployed, people on welfare, and of course, most of my students. Then, as now, it was the dream of these families to move out of the low-lying neighborhoods and climb the hill into neighborhoods closer to the geographic center of the city, like the one where The Care Center was located, and then into the more pristine neighborhoods, like the Highlands.

Wearing a light jacket over my short-sleeve turtleneck sweater and denim skirt, I walked past block after block of Tudors, Victorians, and houses with colonial or Italianate flourishes. But the scenery quickly changed.

Soon I was passing run-down two-family houses and brick apartment buildings. On one corner an empty lot marked the spot where an abandoned building that had become a haven for drug dealers had recently been torn down by the city. On a sunny afternoon earlier that week, a young woman pushing her baby in a stroller just a few blocks from where I was walking had been caught in gunfire between two gangs. That morning's paper reported that she was in stable condition and recovering from a gunshot wound to her leg. The baby was unharmed. Recalling that story, I could feel the breeze tickle my exposed ankles, and I started to wish I'd taken the car.

Another recent story in the local paper told of a young man who murdered his girlfriend's eighteen-month-old baby. The boyfriend, who was not the baby's father, was watching the child while the baby's mother was shopping. A year later, one of my students would write a beautiful poem in memory of her nephew—the baby described in that news report.

When I arrived at the center I had just enough time to put down my bag and rush to the basement classroom for assembly. This was a poor attendance day, which turned out to be a good thing, because even with fewer girls present, the room was packed. Students filled every available chair and others sat on desks and on the floor. Sixty young women were enrolled in the school, but between appointments with doctors or social workers, students' illnesses or their babies'—as well as myriad other trivial or profound reasons—we were lucky to have fifty present on any given day. When all of the students were finally seated, the teachers squeezed in, perching atop the bookshelves along the side and back walls of the room. I leaned against the closed door next to Rhonda.

Today the girls would pick a new slate of afternoon classes. This was one of many ways the center distinguished itself from other GED programs. The mornings were devoted primarily to the subjects that would appear on the GED exam, but the afternoons were for enrichment activities. The director of the school insisted that the students should have the same opportunities as kids who attended prep school. If those students had a crew team, so should ours; if those kids took photography and ceramics, so should ours. The ideal was noble, but its execution often a bit jarring.

"*Permiso*," Ana called out, trying to get the students' attention. "*Con permiso, por favor.*" When the room quieted, she welcomed everyone and then launched into the day's business. "Today you'll choose your afternoon classes, your electives," she told the students, first in English, then in Spanish. The girls were given forms on which they would request their first, second, and third choices. One by one each teacher came to the front of the room to tell the students about the classes they'd be offering. The art teacher, a tall, thin white man wearing thick, black-rimmed glasses, addressed the group in halting Spanish. He explained that in his class the girls would paint murals on the walls of the second floor hallway. Next the computer teacher, an African American woman whose hair fell in a cascade of braids framing her round face, explained that students who chose her class would build their own computers from castoffs. In the end they'd each create a working machine that they could bring home to keep. Next came a yoga instructor, and someone who would teach a drumming class.

"Tzivia," Ana said, motioning me to the front of the room, "will tell you about the writing class."

I stepped forward and looked out over the students, who were anxious for me to finish up so they could check off their choices and go to the lunchroom for the mid-morning snack. Who is going to take writing, I wondered, when they could choose instead to paint the walls or score a free computer?

"If you take my class you'll get a free living room set," I said. A few of the teachers laughed. The girls looked on blankly. "Just kidding," I said. "I'll be teaching autobiography in the afternoon. It'll be a chance for you to write stories about your life." I gave a brief explanation of the class, and returned to my place at the door.

As the students picked up their pens to make their choices, I walked around the room with the other teachers to see if anyone had any questions and to collect the finished papers. As I moved from desk to desk, I could see that almost everyone had chosen computers or art for their first choices.

Afterward, I went upstairs to prepare for my poetry class. I first asked the students if any had taken me up on my challenge to memorize the Browning poem. I had been asking the question nearly every week, and still no one had made the attempt. I wasn't surprised, but I couldn't help feeling disappointed. But rather than dwell on that I plowed ahead. Walt Whitman was my favorite poet and I had brought in a selection from *Leaves of Grass* for the day's lesson. I started by reading from section 6 of "Song of Myself," which contains the lines:

A child said, What is the grass? fetching it to me with full hands,
How could I answer the child? I do not know what it is any
    more than he.

When I looked up from the book I saw that Latisha had taken out her nail clippers and had begun giving herself a manicure. When I asked her to put the clippers away, she shot me daggers with her eyes. She had recently shaved her eyebrows and repainted them with what appeared to be a streak of black mascara, a popular style among my students that year, but one that made Latisha's already intense scowl even more intimidating. "I'm not bothering you," she said.

I couldn't pinpoint when the war between Latisha and me had broken out. All I knew was that in class after class lately she challenged my authority, refused to write, or started conversations with Sylvie while I spoke.

"It's disrespectful to trim your nails while I'm trying to teach. You can do it after class."

She didn't bother looking up. "I have a piece of nail hanging off. I won't be able to listen until I cut it."

I decided to try to ignore her. "Whitman compares the grass to a green handkerchief dropped by God," I said, looking past Latisha to the rest of the students. "What else could we compare it to?"

"Grass is grass," Sylvie offered. "Why you ask us these questions?"

"What might your babies be thinking when they look at the grass?" I prodded.

"That it looks like green paint," Ruth muttered.

"Good," I said. "What else?"

"Like Astroturf?" Marta suggested.

Latisha had put her clippers down and was now fishing in her purse for something else. I handed out paper and asked the class to write about an ordinary object as though they'd never seen it before. As always, just after I gave the assignment Evelyn looked up as if I'd just walked into the room. "What do you want us to do?" she asked.

"I don't mind repeating myself for you," I said with a conspiratorial smile. We'd played out this routine every week for two years now. "The reason I don't mind is because I know it will be worth it when I see what you write." I never knew whether Evelyn really needed to hear instructions twice or whether she just liked the attention. I suspected she was also stalling for time. Despite repeated efforts at the GED exam, her classroom teacher had told me that her scores had barely moved at all.

While the students were busy, I walked over to Latisha's desk and sat in the empty seat next to hers. "Have I done something to offend you?" I asked. "Because the last few times I've seen you, you've seemed angry at me."

"I just don't want to be here, if you want to know the truth. I think school is boring."

Behind her Sylvie snickered.

"Well, then write about where you do want to be. Writing is a great way to go someplace else. Just write. You can choose to share it with me or not." Surprisingly, as I walked away, she picked up her pen and began to work.

I moved on. Ruth was writing—a rare enough event that I felt, momentarily, elated. Then, as I passed Marta's desk I noticed she was trimming *her* nails now.

"Marta, please put that away." She handed the clippers back to Latisha.

Sylvie and Gloria were both writing furiously. Then, just as I was about to ask if anyone would like to read her poem out loud, Yari entered the room. I hadn't seen much of her in the past couple of weeks. Everyone stopped writing and looked up at Yari, who was practically bouncing with excitement. "I passed," she said.

The room broke out into a chorus of congratulations and questions. "You did for real?" Marta asked. "You passed the GED?" she went on, sounding, I thought, more jealous than happy.

"That's fantastic," I told Yari. "I'm sad for me, but very happy for you." Yari had been one of my first students, and I had come to rely on her as the one consistently positive presence in the room. I was very sorry that she'd be leaving our class for good.

"We're almost out of time," I told the group. I knew there was no use trying to continue in the face of the excitement Yari's news had generated. "We'll read these poems next week." I walked around the room and collected the papers. When I got to Evelyn's desk she was painstakingly arranging her poems in her folder. I suspected she was trying to ignore the commotion on the other side of the room. "Can I peek?" I asked, and took the folder from her to read what she had written:

> I am the ocean around the world.
> People die in me
> fish die in me
> it's not my fault.
> I feel the sun burning me.
> In the other side I am freezing.
> I am deep and shallow.[12]

"I love this," I said. "I love that the ocean is deep and shallow at the same time. That people die in it, but it's innocent."

"Yeah, right," she said. "You just like whatever we write." The crowd that had gathered around Yari was becoming louder as more students joined the group. Even Latisha put down her nail polish and went over to talk to her.

"No, I really, really like your poem," I said. I realized now that Evelyn and Yari had started at the center at about the same time. Yari's news must have been painful for her. "Mind if I type it for you?" I asked. I had an agreement with my students that if they wrote something they particularly liked, and if they had worked hard during class, they could put a star on the top of their page and I would type it up for them.

"I didn't put a star on it," she said.

"I see that, but I think you should have."

Back in my office after class, I had to admit to myself that Evelyn was right. I did love nearly everything she and her classmates wrote. Even today, when Latisha had made me furious, I knew that when I opened her poetry folder her words would win me over.

The educator Paulo Freire wrote that education is an act of love, and the effective teacher educates *with* love. As I recalled Freire's words, "It is impossible to teach without the courage to love, without the courage to try one thousand times without giving up. It is impossible to teach without a forged, invented and well-thought out capacity to love,"[13] I had to stop and wonder.

I didn't love my students that day, I admitted to myself. I didn't love them a lot of the time. I could say that I loved them in moments. Like the moment when Rosa recited her poem about pigeons, which it turned out was really a poem about the prostitute on her street:

> ... a pigeon sang
> in my ears as the other pigeon who
> stands on my street corner
> sang in my mailman's ears, "5 dollars
> 5 dollars, 5 dollars."[14]

I loved Susan for one afternoon only: the day she told me she'd written a poem at home. And I loved Esme when she swore, then apologized profusely for her slip, saying, "I'm sorry, Teacher, I can't help that shit." Mostly though, I loved my students in groups. I adored them when they forgot to act like they didn't care and got caught up in creating metaphors and similes with me: *The orange smells like hairspray. It feels as soft as a Downy towel. Loneliness is an empty room full of darkness. Confusion is a caged bird in a jungle.* Hearing their creations I would rush to write each phrase on the board, even though I meant to only record the "good" ones. What I loved were their words.

At the end of each class, I walked through the hall back to my office, stealing glances at their poems before I even shut my door. As I pulled each piece of loose-leaf paper from the students' manila folders, I had the same feeling of expectant pleasure as when I walked barefoot on the beach scooping up handfuls of shells that had washed up on shore, certain I was about to gaze down at a palm full of wonders. The poems and the shells were alike to me; their beauty was more precious for the fact that it was unrevised, unself-conscious, and often unintentional.

That day's poems were odes to ordinary things:

> Hear my wash going da da da
> and the water rinsing zzz
> then drying dum-dum-dum
> the smell of Clorox—strong
> and detergent, a really nice smell…[15]

Sifting through their poems I reveled in the accidental lines. Obedient lines. Reluctant lines. Lines written on demand. They were lines written from the small store of words they knew how to spell, that they thought wouldn't be laughed at. In many cases the authors couldn't have said why they wrote them, or they'd say something very different than anything I might have guessed.

I searched the margins of the pages I was reading for hastily scribbled stars that would alert me to type a poem. I found Evelyn's paper, with the star drawn by my hand. I hesitated for a moment and considered whether the other teachers were right when they'd warned me not to offer this incentive. "Don't be their secretary," one teacher told me. A good teacher would require the students to take their poems to the computer lab and type them themselves, thus encouraging them to practice another essential skill (keyboarding) while learning to follow a piece of writing through from rough draft to finished product. But I *wanted* to type the poems for my students. I justified this indulgence by arguing that it motivates students to write more after they've seen their work cleaned up into the black and white of the printed page. Whether or not this was true no longer mattered to me. I knew by then that typing the poems was a way I could luxuriate in the cadence of their unguarded voices. I could handle the images and phrases like the seashells I pocketed at the beach. I could pick them up and cherish them. I opened a new Word document and quickly typed Evelyn's poem, then three more by other students who'd decorated their poems with a star or the words *Type Please.*

Some parents pull pictures of their children from their wallet every chance they get. If someone was in my office when I was reading my students' work, I'd pull out pieces of blue-lined loose-leaf paper and say, "Listen to this one." When I finished reading that poem I'd pull out another. "There's one more you just have to hear," I'd say, and then another. I read them over the phone to friends. I read them to teachers who merely happened to mention a certain student's name.

This fascination with spontaneous poetry must have started when I was thirteen. I remember noticing on my mother's bookshelves that year a new volume that stood out among the novels by Faulkner, Woolf, Cheever, Irving and the Brontë sisters. I had settled into the butterfly-backed armchair, opened the chunky paperback, and begun to read. The book, *Wishes, Lies and Dreams,* by Kenneth Koch had been published six years earlier in 1970. It contained a collection of poems written by children from a New York City public school where Koch taught. He was experimenting with the notion that children could learn to write poetry. I loved the way words thrown one against another sparked a new idea into being. I loved the repetition of phrases and the bright images that were like first paintings: uncomplicated and surprisingly alive. I loved the poems' unintended perfection.

> Be sure to go to the German Alps and say hello to my Dad
> Eat a lot of apple strudel in Germany
> Maybe you can dig a tunnel and find another tunnel where
>   prisoners are escaping from East Berlin
> Eat all the Italian type spaghetti
> Try making some pizza
> Eat matzoh balls
> Knock down the Leaning Tower of Pisa...[16]

I must have stared with a polished intent at the red apple on the white cover of that book. That apple must have settled someplace deep in my imagination, because I would find it, unexpectedly, again.

When I went to graduate school for creative writing, nearly two decades later, having long forgotten Koch's book, I applied for a work-study job I'd seen posted on a bulletin board in the student lounge. The successful applicant would be a poet in the schools with Teachers and Writers Collaborative—the program, I learned later, that had sponsored Koch's teaching experiment. Having never taught children before, and having no overwhelming desire to do so, I applied for the job anyway because the pay was decent and the hours were convenient. But then, there I was, a teacher in an inner-city public school in New York helping elementary and junior high school kids write poems like the ones in that book. Each evening when I returned to my room, feeling simultaneously high and empty, energized and exhausted, and with my tote bag overflowing with children's poems, I would be nearly breathless with excitement. I was hardly able to wait to sit down before grabbing a handful of poems to see what my students had created. It was as though that book with the apple on the cover was adding to itself, right before my eyes.

I thought I was finished with that job when I completed my MFA, but back home in Massachusetts I realized I missed teaching. Working at The Care Center offered a way to reconnect with that unexpected joy.

Only now it was more difficult to get to that spontaneous wordplay from my students. Teenage girls who had babies in the day care downstairs and boyfriends in the neighborhood, who they said were really nice even though they blackened their eye with a thrown fist or boot, weren't as willing to take off into flights of nonsense as children who wrote lines such as: "The light is a seagull/ Mrs. Wiener is a pretzel she is worth two cents."[17]

I pulled out Latisha's poem:

> Can you imagine my
> mother?
> I can! Imagine
> a black wild cat
> running after me as if I were a mouse.
> As if I owed her
> dinner...[18]

"Wow," I scrawled across the top, momentarily forgetting our mutual animosity, "I love this!"

For the past couple of years I had collected the students' poems, printed them, and distributed the stapled booklets within the school. As part of my new contract, creating an annual anthology of student writings was one of my required duties. This year I would have to come up with something good if I wanted to convince the director that she'd made the right move in hiring me, when in reality I'd have kept teaching there for free.

As I began to contemplate ways I could make this year's collection stand out, I remembered once more the story I'd read with Judith and her class on my first day at the center. Again, I wanted to find it. This time I decided to contact Judith, who might still have the article. I didn't have her phone number, but I found her email address and sent her a message asking if she had a copy, or at least the subject's name so I could look it up on my own. She sent back a reply saying she remembered the article, but she couldn't recall any details, either. "I could go out to the barn and dig around to find it," she wrote. But I didn't want to bother her. I knew she was finishing up work on her degree and searching for a new job.

I decided instead to ask around at the center to see if anyone there could remember the name of the woman who had once inhabited these rooms.

"I don't know her name, but she was a strong, independent woman," the director of the center told me. "I think she was poor, too." Anne was relatively new to her job, though, so she suggested I talk to the head of the day care, who had worked at the center for more than a decade.

The sign on the door to Aida's first-floor office, which was located in the day care, read, "Knock Gently." I barely scraped my knuckles on the wood so as not to wake any sleeping babies. Aida let me in, and leaned back against her desk. "I think her name was Elizabeth," she said. "She was very old and in a wheelchair and one day she fell down the stairs. Every time we hear a strange noise in the building we say, 'There goes the old lady again.'" I must have looked skeptical, because Aida said that if I didn't believe the house was haunted, I should talk to Michelle.

Michelle, the center's financial officer, was known for being practical and efficient. She didn't confine herself to the center's budget: if a light bulb burned out, a paper towel dispenser was jammed, or a new computer needed to be set up, she'd be there ready to fix the problem. Nonetheless, Michelle confirmed that she had heard inexplicable noises while working late in her second-floor office. "I've heard thumping sounds from the third floor as if someone's moving furniture. I've gone upstairs to look, and of course no one's there."

Rather than being frightened, the women who worked in the building said the possibility of the former inhabitant's incorporeal presence there affirmed their own. Ana told me she believed it was no accident the building, once owned by a teen mother who succeeded in life, was now occupied by teen mothers who were fighting to make better lives for themselves and their children. "She wants us here," Ana said.

I called a member of the city's historical commission to see if she knew anything about the woman who had run a publishing company from the house on Cabot Street, but she didn't. She suggested I visit the History Room at the public library.

The History Room. I hadn't even known there was one. At lunchtime I walked back to the library, this time determined to leave with something concrete—if not the article Judith had introduced me to, at least a couple of facts about the woman who once lived in The Care Center. A name, at the very least.

The more this story eluded me, the more I wanted to know it. This time, when I entered the library I walked past the reference room and climbed the stairs to the second floor. When I entered the History Room I found two men looking through a book and talking in a far corner. Inhaling the dust of old books and papers, I crossed the well-worn Oriental carpet to where they were seated. "I'm looking for information about a former inhabitant of 247 Cabot Street, the building where The Care Center is now located," I said.

"We need a name," the older of the two men said, without bothering to look up from the book he was studying.

"I don't have a name. But she was the city's first female councilman and she ran a publishing company right here in Holyoke."

"I can't do much without a name," the older man said. "Go back and get a name."

I was incredulous. How could a woman like this, the publisher of an offbeat journal and the first woman to hold public office in small city, be completely unknown to the keepers of local history? I turned to leave, but then changed my mind. "Don't you have a street index?" I asked. "I could find her name that way."

He replied that there was no street index from the early 1900s, which is when I thought Towne would have lived there. "What about a history of city politics? She'd be mentioned there." Another no. But there were municipal reports, and each one began with a list of city officers. Maybe we could search the lists for a woman's name, I suggested.

The man, who was a library volunteer, finally stopped what he was doing and led me to a shelf of books bound in cracking leather. Each one represented another year in the city's government. I began to search randomly from 1900 on, but quickly realized this would take a lot longer than the span of my lunch hour.

Meanwhile, he found an oversized volume dated January 1936. It was the assessor's record for that year. He gripped the book as though it were a breakfast tray, and placed it on the table in front of me. "It's indexed by street," he said.

I quickly found the address: "247 Cabot Street. Elizabeth Towne, Publisher." Also named were her cook, her maid, and her husband, William E. Towne.

Within minutes the room was abuzz. The volunteer and Devon, the younger man who, it turned out, was in his first week on the job as curator of the History Room, began pulling out files and index cards on Mrs. Towne. I hadn't brought a notebook so I settled at one of the large wooden tables and began scribbling notes on scraps of paper from my handbag. I paged through yellowing newspaper articles and old letters. In the back of a file I found it: a copy of the article Judith had handed out to her class three years before.

"Look at her now, she's soaring," the volunteer said. "And we were just going to toss her out of here."

When I returned to work I climbed the stairs as students poured past me on their way to their afternoon classes. When I reached my third-floor office, the room Michelle had identified as the source of the mysterious, ghostly noises, I pulled out from my tote bag the copy

I had made of the article I'd finally found, sat at my desk, and began to read.

Towne's story, I thought, would be an inspiration for my students. The similarities were obvious: Elizabeth Towne was a teen mother. The students who now occupied her house were teen mothers. In Towne's day, her house was a refuge of sorts for young women. In fact, her habit of hiring young, inexperienced workers and training them to be more skilled won her residence the nickname of "The High School Annex." The same nickname could be applied to The Care Center, an alternative school that welcomed with open arms the poor, pregnant, and disaffected students that the public high school, located just a half mile down the street, had in some way failed. Towne described herself as pulling herself out of poverty and propelling herself into success, and the teens at the center were struggling to do the same.

But the comparisons broke down quickly. Towne was a teen mother in an age when women routinely married young and started families. Even in her day dropping out of school at age fourteen, as Towne had, was unusual but not unheard of—especially not for a girl. Besides, Towne herself would be the first to admit that her formal education didn't begin or end in the schoolroom. She lived in a house filled with books and magazines and was thereby in a position to educate herself.

Meanwhile, the apartments my students lived in, no matter how sparse the furnishings, tended to feature large-screen televisions (albeit of poor quality) and stacks of cheap but impressive-looking electronic equipment, including curvaceous boom boxes and sleek DVD players. But it was rare, if not impossible, to find a book, even a paperback, which would cost a fraction of the price of a DVD.

Unlike Towne, it was the rare student who was legally married, although some referred to their boyfriends as husbands. Maybe because of the fear that welfare would chase the young man down for child support payments he couldn't make, and maybe because he was more likely to come and visit with a bag full of baby clothes or a package of Pampers if left alone, the mothers didn't marry or even live with their baby's fathers. In fact, it was most common for a young woman to refer to this young man, not in relation to herself (i.e., "my boyfriend," "my lover," or even "my husband"), but instead as he was connected to the baby: "my baby daddy" was the way I usually heard the young women refer to their current or former partners.

Poverty, for Towne, was a fleeting condition—one that had no past and little chance of taking hold in the future. For her, being without money was a distasteful state, one that could be conquered with a little gumption, a lucky marriage, and a family loan. For my students, poverty was the only inheritance they had ever known. It was a generations-long snare—a culture and a way of life. Referred to by politicians as a "safety net," the welfare system was most certainly a trap. It was a labyrinth that confounded and confused its victims with rules that seemed to change and transfigure so swiftly as to mesmerize, then paralyze, those condemned to trying to decipher them. Besides, because their own mothers, aunts, and sisters never seemed to find a way out, poverty took on the appearance of a room with no exit.

The more apt comparison, it turned out, was between Elizabeth Towne and me. Granted, the obvious biographical data didn't match up: I had finished not only high school but also college and graduate school, and had never married. But like Towne, I was a white woman who loved to learn, write, and publish. My bookshelves were filled with New Age and self-help books, the genres for which Towne was a founding foremother. Not only that, but I was also the author of just such a book, a collection of short essays about living with spiritual intention and a positive outlook. Ever since I was the age my students were now, I had called myself a feminist, and I admired outspoken women like Towne who fought for women's rights. Inspired by the similarities, I sat down and made a list of things I had in common with Towne, and easily filled an entire, single-spaced page, top to bottom: Elizabeth Towne lived at 247 Cabot Street; I worked at 247 Cabot Street. Elizabeth Towne was a writer; I was a writer as well. Elizabeth Towne was known as the apostle of happy living; I was known at The Care Center as the Happy Teacher. Elizabeth Towne was born beside the Pacific Ocean. I was born within miles of the Atlantic...

A list of things I had in common with my students was much more difficult to complete, and I found myself relying on obvious, nearly universal qualities: We were all female. We lived in the same city at the same point in history. We were all mothers...

The differences even there were so great as to destroy any bridge

I had hoped to construct. We were all female, but they were also Latina and poor, and part of a culture that placed different demands on women. We were all mothers, but I, as a lesbian co-parent, never experienced pregnancy or birth firsthand. We lived in the same city, but in my neighborhood people had lawns and gardens—and gardeners. We were contemporaries of one another, but couldn't find a single movie or popular singer that we liked in common.

Tommyrot! I could hear Mrs. Towne protest. *If you focus all of your mind's energy on your differences you will only serve to expand them. Focus instead on the threads you share in common and you will discover the ties that bind you together. Lean close, dearie, there is no one to blame for your condition but yourself.*

When I began collecting facts about Elizabeth Towne, I organized my notes into a timeline: 1865—Born. 1880—first marriage to Joseph Holt Struble (a very nice wedding with lots of presents according to a brief memoir). 1898—starts a magazine (with financial support from her father). 1900—divorced her first husband and moved to Holyoke to marry William Elmer Towne. Her timeline also included buying a house, traveling to Europe, sending her son to Lehigh University, becoming the minister of the Church of Truth, running for public office, and writing and publishing dozens of books and pamphlets.

During the autobiography class I was teaching one afternoon a week, I asked my students to make timelines of their lives. I handed out sheets of blue paper, each with a long horizontal line stretching from end to end like a clothesline. Key events in their lives were to be marked on that line, along with a date and short explanation written below. Jazmin began to fill hers in. She made a tick mark at 1990: "Age six, birthday party. My last one. My father died that day." She continued: "Age eight, molested by my brother's friend...Age ten, mother loses custody."

Another student told me she'd moved nine times but she didn't write where she had moved or when. When I prodded her to include on her timeline as many addresses as she could remember, she said, "Okay, but I don't want to list the shelters."

"This is your life story," I argued, "and the shelters are part of your story, so put them in."

Marta filled in the date she was born; the day a month later when she was rushed back to the hospital because she had stopped breathing; the year that she turned five and was taken away from her parents, who were both addicted to heroin, and placed in her grandmother's custody. Then there was the date, somewhere in her ninth-grade year, when she lost her virginity, and the date she found out she was pregnant. Her timeline went on to chronicle the dates that marked her grandmother's slow death from diabetes: "How do you spell amputate?" she asked.

Students filled in their first kisses: stolen in the coat closet of a kindergarten classroom, offered longingly on the stoop of a building, or taken without permission by cousins, uncles, or neighborhood boys. Not one of my students' timelines included a wedding. Nearly all included the funeral of a close relative who had died before reaching old age. Many included the dates when fathers, boyfriends, or brothers went to jail.

After we finished our timelines I asked the class to write about the first home they could remember, whether it was an apartment, an aunt's house, or a shelter. "Include as much detail as you can: what you saw, what you heard, what you felt—everything."

Pens hovered above pages of loose-leaf paper. A few students wrote their names on top of the paper, then slowly added the date.

"Are you stuck?" I asked Marta.

"No," she said. "I just don't wanna think about that stuff."

I'd taught writing workshops to people of all ages, from adults to college students to children, and early memories had always been among the more popular topics. But in this class, it wasn't until we progressed to the teen years, when the girls could write about their pregnancies, or when I asked them to write the story of their babies' births, that the writing began to flow.

During one class I asked my students to think back to when their lives really began. "Was it at your birth?" Some heads nodded tentatively. "Are you sure? Maybe we should begin farther back. Perhaps your life really began at conception?" I suggested. "Or maybe, we should go back even farther, to when your parents met or even your grandparents?" I prompted. No one looked convinced. One student insisted her life began, not when her mother became pregnant, but when *she* did. I looked around. Another student nodded. "Yeah," Jazmin agreed. A chorus of nodding heads and sounds of assent told me that for these young women the utter loss of control in childhood was partly healed by giving birth, by finally being the adult in charge.

Week after week I tried to help students reconstruct on paper their early lives. For one class, I brought in a series of small plastic bags, each filled with a cotton ball soaked in something with a distinct scent: lemon juice, suntan lotion, medicine, peppermint, or whiskey. Smell is the sense most intimately connected with memory, so I handed out the bags and asked the students to take a whiff of the contents, and then write anything that came to mind. The smell of cherry cough syrup sparked Lourdes's imagination. After that class she was captivated by the project of autobiography. While her classmates moaned and complained that they didn't want to think about those times, Lourdes leaned over her paper as if she were alone in the room.

One day Lourdes asked if she could write her entire autobiography with me. She wanted to get her life story on paper, and she needed more time than we had in class. As a result, each Monday at the start of second period, I would go to her basement classroom and pick her up. We climbed the three flights back up to my office with minimal conversation. She would take my chair at the desk while I pulled her folder from the bottom file drawer and showed her that I'd typed her writing from the previous week and written comments on her hand-written draft. After she'd been writing for twenty minutes or so, I'd go into the staff kitchen and microwave a bag of popcorn. When I returned, I'd open the steaming bag and we'd take handfuls of popcorn and discuss what she'd written that day.

It took months for her to produce six pages. Our progress was hampered by her frequent absences, but we managed to establish a workable routine. I tried to get her to focus on details, like the fact that she spent the last month of her pregnancy sleeping on a couch in her mother's apartment because there was no bed for her. But Lourdes tended toward broad descriptions. "I was nervous and scared" summed up her reaction to everything from having sex for the first time at age fifteen, to finding out she was pregnant at sixteen, to leaving her parents' house to live with a boy she barely knew.

Lourdes grew up in Michigan. She'd moved to Holyoke recently, to live with an uncle and, she hoped, to start a new life. Her mother was addicted to drugs and Lourdes lived in the spaces of hope between bottoms. She began her autobiography with the story about how, as a child, she climbed onto the bathroom sink to look in the mirror and found her mother's drug works.

Most days, Lourdes dressed for school in a loose T-shirt, the jacket from a running suit, a denim skirt that covered her knees, and a pair of five-inch heels as thick as towers. She wore her heavy black hair twisted into a bun. When she spoke, her voice started high in her throat and never quite settled down. Everything she said sounded like some form of "*ay*," as in "*ay caramba*." Lourdes was Pentecostal. When I told her I was Jewish she asked, "What's that?"

During a class in which we read poems about hope and despair by author and former inmate Jimmy Santiago Baca and Emily Dickinson ("Hope is the thing with feathers..."), Lourdes wanted only to talk about apocalypse. She opened her Bible to Revelations and tried to convince her classmates that the end could be as near as tomorrow. There was increasing talk of war and as if to prepare us for the random horrors that were to come, that fall the news was full of stories of a mysterious sniper in Washington, D.C. who was targeting people as they went about their daily business, getting into their cars in parking lots, or filling up at gas stations.

Lourdes began her poem: "Hope is Jesus/ Hope is faith." She ended with the lines, "I hope the world will end soon/ so I could go up to Jesus/ and there would be no more danger/ of sinning."

"What about your daughter?" I asked. "Don't you hope the world will keep turning so she can grow up?"

"No," Lourdes answered. "She'll just go down the wrong path at some point and then she'll be going to Hell, too."

After she left school that day, Lourdes went home to the shelter where she'd been living for the past few months. She would be alone that night because her two-year-old daughter was on a court-mandated visit with her father, who was still living in Detroit. Lourdes would wake in the night to the sounds of other women coming and going in the beds around her. She would stare into the not-quite-dark, hoping—but also not hoping—that the world would hold off from ending, at least for a few more days, at least until Tuesday, so she could see her daughter again.

A month or two later, Lourdes stopped coming to school. I asked her counselor where she had gone; I wanted to mail her the pages of the autobiography she had started. But after a few months with no sign of her, I put her folder back into a drawer with dozens of others I kept for students who had left the center suddenly, and without providing their forwarding address. I kept them all in the hopes that someday our paths would cross and I could give them back their words.

Autobiography[19]

It was 1983. My parents were married, having the time of their life. My mom was on birth control but she got pregnant anyways. My grandma told her don't worry, "As long as I'm alive I'll always help you."

In 1984 I was born. My dad was with someone else by then. When I was about 1½ years old my grandma and uncle were shot and killed. My grandma, the one who promised to help, was gone.

When I was five my mom met someone new. I remember him opening the door for her when they were going into the store. I remember getting jealous when I used to see him being so nice to her.

One day I was in the bathroom and I wanted to look in the mirror. But I was too short so I climbed on the sink and stood up and I remember seeing a little tequila bottle, the individual size with a straw coming out the side and aluminum foil with holes on the top and a rubber band holding it on. That's when I realized my parents were doing drugs.

They used to lock themselves in the room. I remember worrying, hoping they were OK. I remember one day me and my mom hid in the closet because the landlord came to pick up the rent money and we didn't have it. When I was 10 years old my mom had my sister and we moved to Detroit. Things were looking good. My parents stopped doing drugs. We had an apartment. My stepfather was working. But then my mom started doing drugs again. She disappeared. The police found her after three days. Then she finally stopped doing drugs. At least we thought she did.

When I was 13 she had my brother. He almost died when he was born. He had tubes going in and out of his body. My stepfather put a picture of my brother next to the Bible and took the liquor that was on top of the refrigerator and poured it down the sink and told God that if his son lived he would never drink again.

After a few months he started drinking again. My mom started doing drugs. I dropped out of school. It wasn't a happy time for any of us.

When I was 14 we moved to Kirkwood Street. The next summer I was 15. I was walking three houses down to my friend's house. And the second house down from mine there was this guy on the porch. I thought he was cute. When he would look in my eyes I would get real nervous and look the other way. A few days later I went to the store and he was following me. He stopped me and asked for my number but instead I got his. The next day I called him. Later that day we seen each other. I remember him coming up to me and giving me a kiss on the cheek. I thought it was so sweet.

A few weeks later we went on a date. It was my first date. I started getting ready at 6:30 p.m. He didn't come to pick me up till 9:30 p.m. I remember him telling me he loved me and then trying to have sex with me. I didn't want to. I never had sex before. He was 20, I was 15. To him it was nothing. For me it was everything. I used to tell him that I didn't want to do anything till I was married but he didn't care. So finally I gave in. I told my mom so I could get birth control. She told my stepfather. He told me he didn't want me at home anymore and that I had to leave.

In September I moved in with my boyfriend and his family. On the third night I was sleeping and I turned to my other side and noticed my boyfriend wasn't next to me. I looked at the clock. It was 3:21 a.m.

I went back to my parents' house. I wanted to get my GED so I started going to this place called the Covenant House. There I met this guy, Benji. He's Christian so I would visit the church he goes to. We would go to church and school together. Then he got a job so I had to drop out of Covenant House because I didn't have a ride anymore. Things started to get serious between us. Two weeks later I was pregnant. We went to the pharmacy and with six dollar bills and three dollars in change we bought a pregnancy test. I took it and it came out positive. I didn't want to tell my mom, but I knew if I hid it, it was going to be worse.

So we went to my mom's house. He waited outside while I went in and told her. She didn't even say anything. I think she was shocked.

Later that night I talked to him on the phone. The next day he told me his parents knew. He said they were listening to us on the phone. He told me to pack my things—that I was going with him. I left my parents without saying bye.

I remember being in the car and having tears fall down my face. I was nervous, scared, but I knew that's what I had to do. I didn't want to be with him but I had no choice because I was pregnant.

I remember when I went to my doctor's appointment to find out if it's a boy or a girl. I was happy and nervous. When we left the doctor's, Benji was mad because they told us I was having a girl. I remember the ride home. He was serious. I asked him if everything was okay. He wouldn't answer me. He didn't talk to me for a week.

He started hanging out with his friends a lot. He would come home from work, take a shower and leave. We would argue sometimes. One day I asked him if he loved me and he said "no."

I told him I wanted to go home. He didn't argue. He took me back to my parents' house. I was a month away from giving birth. He didn't help me carry my boxes or suitcases. He called a few times, but that was all.

One night, I was lying on the couch in my mother's apartment and I couldn't sleep. I'd always thought I wouldn't turn out like the other girls I knew who got pregnant and ended up back in their mother's house. I was going to do it different.

CHAPTER FOUR

BRUJAS

THE CLASSROOM WAS DECKED OUT FOR HALLOWEEN with fake cob-webs, large plastic spiders, and cardboard cutouts of leaning tomb-stones. I handed out copies of Shakespeare's Sonnet 116 and asked the class to look over the poem.

"This one may be a little difficult," I warned them.

"Then why are you giving it to us?" Esme shot back.

"That's a good question," I said, as if I were a professor in tweeds and an undergrad had offered a gem to ponder. "Do you remember your dreams?" I asked her.

Esme rolled her eyes. "Forget it. Let's just read the damn poem."

"No, really, do you remember them?"

"Yes, I remember my stupid dreams."

"Do you understand them?"

She shook her head. "No, my dreams are whack."

"But they make you feel something, right? Maybe scared, maybe happy, maybe sad?"

"Worried," she answered.

"Okay. You see, sometimes we experience things with parts of our mind that aren't logical. Poems make you feel things, or think about things that you may or may not fully understand."

"Okay, I see you're saying something. Now can we read the poem?"

"Not quite yet," I said, enjoying the fact that Esme was now beg-ging to read a poem.

I tried to introduce the class to the idea of Shakespearean English. "Language is like fashion; it changes through history. For example, if I walked in here today wearing a hoop skirt and a frilly blouse, you'd think I looked a little strange, but you'd still know me, right?" A few girls laughed. Latisha rolled her eyes. "Well, it's the same with this poem. We don't use a lot of these words anymore, but we can still recognize the main idea behind them."

"What's the title mean?" Sylvie asked.

"The title is Sonnet 116. Does anyone remember the word *sonnet*?" No one registered any sign of recognition. "Remember the poem I asked you to try to memorize?" I coached. I didn't bother to ask if anyone had learned Browning's poem by heart. "That was a sonnet," I said. "So what does the word mean?"

Luz, a new student who'd taken a seat in the back left corner of the room, looked up. She was thin and had widely spaced eyes. Speaking aloud in class, or even face to face in the lunchroom or hallway, seemed to cause her physical pain. Still, I could see that she had something to say.

"Luz," I asked, "what do you think?"

She winced, as if I'd thrown a dart in her direction. "Song," she whispered.

"Song!" I repeated, unable to mask my enthusiasm. I'd have been happy— no, thrilled—if a student had merely ventured that a sonnet was a kind of poem. "Have you heard this word before?" I asked her. She shook her head from side to side.

"Well, you're right, anyway. The word *sonnet* comes from the Latin root *son*, which means 'song' or 'sound.'"

"It just sounded like song," Luz muttered.

"Good. You have an excellent ear, and that will help you a lot with poetry," I said.

A sonnet, I reminded them, is a rhyming poem containing fourteen lines. "There's more to it, too," I said, "but we'll talk about that later. Now, back to Shakespeare. What other words do we need to learn?"

"Admit," Sylvie called out.

"Impediments," Suleika added.

"Alters?" Evelyn asked.

I wrote each word on the board, but could barely keep up. "What does he mean by 'remover'?" Esme asked. Soon, out of a fourteen-line poem of fewer than seventy-five different words, there were fourteen that needed to be defined. It is a basic rule when teaching new readers that if a page of writing has more than ten words that need to be defined for a class, the text is probably too challenging for that group.

"This is way too hard," Esme complained. She was saying outright what I felt some of the teachers at the center had been hinting at. They kept leaving poems in my mailbox or on my desk by Nuyorican or other spoken-word poets, along with little sticky notes that said things like, "Your students might like this," or "this is something the girls might relate to." I suspected they thought I was pushing dead white male poetry on these young, very much alive Latinas. But I felt compelled to keep bringing in poems by Shakespeare, Keats, Rossetti, Frost, and Bishop. If I didn't, I feared, they might never find them.

"Why don't you bring us poems we can understand?" Suleika said with an air of exasperation.

"You ladies are definitely smart enough for this poem." I looked at the clock. I'd be lucky if we had ten minutes at the end of class to write by the time we'd gotten through reading. "Everyone turn your papers over. I'm going to recite the poem to you now, and I want you to listen to it as if it's a song on the radio. When you listen to the radio you don't care if you understand every word, do you?" Heads nodded. "Right, you understand the mood even if you don't understand every syllable. So just listen to this poem and tell me how it makes you feel. What do you think Shakespeare was thinking about when he wrote it?" I recited the poem slowly, trying to feel my way through it. I concluded with the lines: "If this be error and upon me proved, / I never writ, nor no man ever loved."

"That was nice," Sylvie whispered when I was done.

"It sounded phat, but I still don't know what the fuck he's talking about," Esme said.

"It's about love," Luz said. "The forever kind."

"That's it!" I said.

"I never had the forever kind of love," Gloria sighed.

"Well, that's something you can write about," I said, and began handing out sheets of paper.

—

The students were gone for the day, and our staff meeting had just ended. I was packing my papers into my bag, getting ready to leave. Rhonda sat at one of the desks in the third-floor classroom, where the meeting had been held, finishing the remains of the pork fried rice she'd ordered from a neighborhood Chinese restaurant. Meanwhile, she and Ana were discussing a scheduling conflict concerning the new athletics classes that Rhonda was organizing.

"You'd have to use some of your *bruja* powers to make *that* work," Rhonda joked, reviewing Ana's plan.

"What does *bruja* mean?" I asked, putting my bag over my shoulder, getting ready to leave. The Spanish word had appeared in three different student poems that week. When I asked the girls what it meant they would break into animated debates in Spanish, arguing over the precise translation.

"A *bruja* is like a witch," Ana explained. "They cast spells. For example, if you want a man to be under your power, you write his name on a piece of paper and put it in your shoe." She went on with a list of other spells a *bruja* could work: to make someone fall in love with you, write their name on a piece of paper, fill a glass with water and cover it with a plate on which you've placed the paper and turn the whole thing over without spilling the water. If you are having a spate of bad luck and need to change your fortune, wear your underwear inside out. And if you have to be exorcised of a bad spirit, take off all your clothes, wrap yourself in a towel, and have the *bruja* dance around you. At this point in her litany, Ana lunged at me as I stood in frozen surprise. She began dancing around me, flapping her hands in front of her chest.

"Are you a *bruja*?" I asked after she stopped.

"No, no," Ana said, reaching over to pull a tissue from the box on the teacher's desk and wiping her forehead with it. "I'm a Christian," she insisted.

"But you're not *just* a Christian. You really do this stuff," I ventured.

"No," Ana insisted. "It's in my *lineage*."

"So your grandmother did this and you watched?"

"Yes," Ana said, finally conceding that she was a nonpracticing *bruja*. "I walk into rooms and I sense spirits," she said.

"Do you feel spirits here, in this house?" I asked.

"Definitely," she said.

"Whose?"

"Elizabeth's. I sense her in here. She wants us here. We've tried to move this school so many times to different locations, and every time the deal falls through. Elizabeth has decided we have to stay."

I remembered the time Ana told me that she believed the center was meant to be in the house at 247 Cabot Street. She'd said that Elizabeth Towne wanted us there. But I hadn't realized she had meant it literally, that she believed Towne's ghost actually had a role in this.

A few minutes later the pre-GED teacher, V, came back into the room. (We called her by the first letter of her last name to avoid confusion, because her first name was Carmen, and there were at least five other Carmens working or studying at the center at that time.) "I was just telling Tzivia about *brujas*. You know about that stuff, too."

"Oh, sure," V said. She explained that she never gets any sleep because she's too busy fighting off demons. "For a while when I'd be sleeping with my husband I'd feel another presence in the bed between us. I could smell her, like tobacco, like cigars. Then I found out a woman was interested in him. She was trying to push me out of the picture."

Sury, one of the teachers for the Spanish-speaking students, walked by just then. "How about you?" I asked her. "Are you a *bruja*, too?"

Sury's English was limited, and she didn't understand my question. Ana answered instead. "No, not her, she's more European. She looks down on this sort of thing." Sury looked on without expression, so V translated my question into Spanish for her.

"No, no," she answered with a smile. "Not a *bruja*."

"See," Ana said, looking satisfied. "I can tell. I can tell about people right away."

"Can Anglos be *brujas*?" I asked.

Ana considered my question seriously. "Sure," she said, "why not."

"Then what about me," I said. "Am I a *bruja*?"

"You?" She turned and faced me, her brown eyes boring into mine for a long instant. "You," she repeated. "You have too many walls around you. Many, many walls. No one can pass through and see inside. I really can't read you."

I laughed, trying to keep the conversation light. But Ana just kept looking at me with a serious expression. "I'm right, aren't I?" she asked.

I turned to Elizabeth Towne for advice. Not because Ana's comment disturbed me—although it did. I knew without her telling me that at The Care Center I felt constrained, unable to be myself—and yet at the same time, it was in that house that I felt closest to my heart's desires. I loved poetry, I loved teaching. I could identify, if not with my students' poverty and early pregnancies, then with their youth, their anger, their pride, and their willingness to be transformed. But something was missing. Something was keeping me from connecting with them, with the staff, and even with the poems. But what was it?

If I had the powers of a *bruja*, I would write the question on a piece of paper, as Ana advised, and put it under a glass of water or on the bottom of my shoe.

Or, I could ask Mrs. Towne's advice. For starters, I wanted to know how I could find *her*. I wanted to learn the details of her life, but all she would tell me in the articles and pamphlets I had dug up was that I should wash my face with lemon juice, meditate for a half hour every morning, and practice breathing in long, slow draughts that filled my solar plexus. I should remain cheerful at all times, eliminate meat from my diet, and eat fruit and nuts instead. I should take a walk every day in any weather, and I should leap from bed as soon as my eyes opened in the morning and begin the day at full throttle. One thing I learned from her, however, did help me with my quest to unlock the story of her life.

Towne, I discovered, believed that planning one's day according to what *had* to be done was spiritually deadening. Instead, she insisted, one should get in tune with what she called one's "spiritual tides," or desires.

"Perhaps you will ask me *how* and where I *feel* these spiritual tides," Towne wrote in her autobiographical self-help book, *Experiences in Self-Healing.* "Well, dearie, I feel them *in my desires,* in my 'moods.' I follow these inclinations religiously, in full faith that I am working *with* spiritual tides in the universe."

She wasn't handing me the pages of her autobiography, but Towne was, I felt, giving me permission to submit to my desire to spend every lunch hour at the library reading through her papers, taking notes, and making out interlibrary loan requests for more books and articles that contained information by or about her.

But despite the mark she'd left on the New Thought movement internationally, she seemed to have left only the faintest of impressions on the city's history. When I began visiting the library's History Room, they had only a small handful of her magazines, which I studied in depth. But where were the rest of the issues? Towne had published *Nautilus* monthly for more than fifty years. There should be more than 600 issues archived in Holyoke. Instead, there were fewer than a dozen.

Still, I was able to begin to piece together a sketchy biography of her life. The lack of details I unearthed both frustrated and captivated me. For example, the fact that I knew so little about her relationship with her second husband, William, allowed me plenty of room to speculate. From pictures I could see that he had been a thin, handsome man with a kind face. From the handful of articles I found I knew that about a year before he met Elizabeth, William had moved to Holyoke from Walpole, New Hampshire. Ten years Elizabeth's junior, William worked as a stenographer for Albion Paper and had begun his own business selling New Thought literature on the side. He even published some of his own articles in New Thought publications. He and Elizabeth met through a series of letters they exchanged about his desire to advertise in her publication, and he began to contribute some articles to *Nautilus*. When she came to Holyoke to meet him for the first time, Elizabeth stepped off the train and she and William proceeded directly to the First Congregational church, where they were married by Reverend G.W. Winch.

I was in awe of the certainty of William's gesture, and of Elizabeth's willingness to pack up everything and travel thousands of miles to join a man she had known only through his written words. That they never had children together caught my imagination, too. On the one hand, I was glad for them—for Elizabeth especially. She was thirty-five when they married and probably felt too old to start again with babies. It must have been a relief for her to have a relationship as an adult with no children to distract her. But what about William? Did he regret never being a father? Did their childlessness point to a lack of intimacy between them?

According to at least one account, William never visited Elizabeth at the end of her life, during the final four months she spent in a nursing home. He would have been in his mid-eighties by that time, which could simply mean he was too frail to make the twelve-mile trip to Springfield to see his wife. But was there something else, too? What happened during their sixty years together?

After Elizabeth's death, all records of William, and of her children, Catherine and Chester, seemed to disappear from Holyoke's history. The house, I learned from the city's Registry of Deeds, was sold soon after Elizabeth died, not passed down to one of the children or grandchildren.

The answers, I thought, would be in her personal papers. Surely such a prolific writer kept a journal and saved her correspondence. But who had her diaries? Her bundles of letters? Where had her furniture gone? Her desk? Her Dictaphone? Everything seemed simply to have disappeared.

"When a man or a woman knows where they are going, the whole world moves out of their way," Elizabeth Towne had written in the *Nautilus* some ninety-seven years before. Everything she said sounded profound to me now. It wasn't so much the depth of her thought that moved me, but the fact that her words had managed to survive the stretch of years.

I had never particularly cared for history; I wasn't drawn to old things in general. I liked books in their latest edition, folded into crisp paper jackets. I didn't shop in antique stores, because I favored furniture with no signs of wear, and I had no need for aged cheeses or vintage wines. But now I was seeing what the incubator of time was capable of. I was feeling how rich the soil of accumulated years could be if you sank a spade of inquiry into its layers.

Now, with Mrs. Towne's ghost at my side, walking through the halls of The Care Center had become an experience charged with new excitement. I'd wander into my coworkers' offices and admire the pressed tin ceiling or peer out the windows and imagine how the view had changed since Mrs. Towne's time. I stood in Karen, the bookkeeper's, office one afternoon trying to decide whether this had been Elizabeth's private office, based on a description she'd written of looking out a south-facing window to a magnolia tree in bloom. I was so engrossed in my mission that I didn't notice anyone entering the room, nor did I realize Karen was standing behind me, eyeing my back, as I gazed over her filing cabinets and out the window. When I finally registered her presence, it didn't occur to me to apologize or explain myself. In that moment I was in Elizabeth's room, not hers.

"What kind of tree is that?" I asked pointing across the lawn.

"I have no idea," Karen said.

"A magnolia, maybe?"

"No, it's definitely not a magnolia," she said.

Had I been paying attention, I would have noted the impatience in her voice. But I didn't. I was in the distracted state of someone in love. It *was* love, in a sense—I was falling into a historical infatuation.

As with the early weeks and months of a new relationship, every detail I discovered about Towne was a gem to be cherished. Elizabeth Towne designed her own practical dresses for working in the garden, I'd tell my partner at dinner. Or I'd wake up thinking about whether Towne would have driven or walked to her lunches at the Roger Smith House downtown, or whether she'd have been friends with Belle Skinner, the philanthropist and daughter of the city's great silk manufacturer who had lived across the street.

Towne had been described as radiating love, as "glowing from an inner light." She was said to have had "snapping eyes and a quick tongue," to have been "tall, impressive and imposing."[20] She was "a champion of new ideas for a better world."[21] And I was standing in her house.

"Were you looking for something?" Karen finally asked.

Jolted out of my reverie, I told her I wasn't, turned, and climbed the stairs to my own office.

I faced my bookshelf in search of inspiration. I was looking for a poem I might teach that week. I began with my favorites: Whitman, Plath, Dickinson, Frost, Brooks. But now, every time I read a line I'd have Esme's voice in my head. "What are all those fancy words for? Why can't he just say what he means?"

I began to feel smothered by the number of words, allusions, and expressions I knew my students wouldn't understand. During recent classes I'd had to explain who Snow White was, and to define the words *riddle, dazzle* and *emerald.* After reading them Whitman's "O Captain! My Captain!" I had to explain what the Civil War was, but was heartened when Ruth raised her hand and said she knew how Abraham Lincoln had died. "Good, Ruth," I said. "How did he die?"

"He got shot at while he was watching a movie," she explained. I hated the idea of ruining the moment for her, but I was compelled to explain that in those days theaters were for watching plays, because movies had not yet been invented.

I considered Frost, but feared they wouldn't be able to relate to the image of a man working in an orchard picking apples all day long and into the evening. Could they get past phrases like "a wooden way regardless sown" to understand Dickinson's meditation on suffering? I picked out a poem by Sylvia Plath. They'd enjoy her rage and her pain, I thought.

> Daddy, I have had to kill you.
> You died before I had the time –
> Marble-heavy, a bag full of God,
> Ghastly statue with one grey toe…

Esme's voice seemed to be blasting in my ear: "What is this shit?" And I closed the book.

I pulled out another and another. The clipped cadences, enunciated alliterative phrases, allusions groomed and gleaned from the finest editions of the most pedigreed books—once a comfort, they seemed cruel to me now.

I wanted to teach Yeats, Stevens, Stein. They wanted "Poetry for the Teenage Soul." Sure, we made it through Shakespeare's sonnet, but was I really making them feel stupid instead of smart? Last week I'd asked the class if there were any poets they'd *want* to read, and Marta said Maya Angelou. At her age I loved Maya Angelou, too, I reminded myself. But I couldn't bear the thought of another discussion of "I Know Why the Caged Bird Sings" or "Still I Rise." But, I reminded myself, Esme might like it.

Esme had a baby boy and a man who she said was always by her side. Last year, before she became a mother, all Esme wanted was to party. She was into all the wrong things, and one day a cop pulled over the car she was riding in, and found a gun under her seat. Now, Esme had a record, but it wasn't too late, she told herself, to do things right.

At night all she wanted now was to watch her baby sleep. She would prefer to bring him in to class instead of leaving him in the day care, she said again and again.

When I asked her what kinds of poems she'd like to read, she said she liked something that makes her laugh or cry, as long as it does something. She'd like to write a poem, she said when I complained about the blank page on her desk, but first she wanted to know where the periods go.

I decided finally to teach Maya Angelou and recite a poem by Plath, just to recite it. We didn't have to discuss it; they didn't have to understand. The strategy seemed to work. In class that week Esme wrote, stretching out her own poem by throwing in some lines of Angelou's. "That's okay," I told her, and I showed her how she could acknowledge Angelou's influence in the poem's epigraph. "In poetry it's not considered stealing when you use another poet's lines; it's called 'being inspired.'"

Esme thought about poetry's loophole for stealing, then asked whether, when she stole her boyfriend right out from under his former woman's gaze, that was being inspired, too?

I told her to stop talking and write about it, and she did. "It was a hot summer afternoon and he was parked by the curb," Esme wrote. His woman was looking down from three stories above. Under her gaze, Esme walked up to the driver's side and asked for a light. They've been together ever since.

"Can I use the word *bitch* in my poem?" Esme wanted to know.

"In poetry you want to pick the best word for the job. You should use original, surprising words. That one's kind of overused." Esme looked at me as if I were speaking in tongues. "I'm just asking you to give it some thought. Think about what you *really* want to say," I concluded.

Esme held her pen above the page as if it were a fork poised above a plate of hot food, and she was impatient to eat. "I wanna say *bitch*," she said simply, and proceeded to write.

———

The days were growing shorter and darkness was making its seasonal descent. Another Republican governor had just been inaugurated in Massachusetts, and those of us working with disenfranchised people knew what that meant: budget cuts. For our students that would mean fewer services, more pressure to move off welfare quickly, fewer beds in the homeless shelters where several of our students now lived ... and we could only imagine what else. For staff, it meant our jobs might not be there in another six or twelve months.

Some of the teachers at the center had encouraged the students to vote, driving them to the polls and using newspaper articles about the elections as reading material during class. When they heard that the Republican candidate had won the election, one of my students suggested we invite him to our school, so he could see how hard they were working and so he could see the faces of the people whom his budget cuts would hurt.

Suleika cocked an arm over the putty-colored plastic back of her chair. "He wouldn't *infest* himself with us," she declared. I admired her poetic turn of the word *infest*, and the dramatic way she nearly spit the syllables at the absent politician. But the conversation about politics quickly turned into a shouting match over whether women on welfare, present company excluded, were indeed lazy. Then a specific insult against a young woman, whom they all seemed to know, was flung into the mix.

"Ladies," I shouted. "That's enough!" The argument, which I could no longer follow, because the students had all slipped into Spanish, quieted but did not cease altogether. "I'm not going to be the Happy Teacher today," I said. Now they were silent. "I need you to take turns talking in class. And I need you to stay on the subject. I'm serious about this today, and I really will ask anyone who can't follow this simple instruction to leave."

There was a comma's width of silence, then a low roar of giggles. I kept my face serious, even as I tried to decode the change in mood.

"You can't get mad," Gloria said.

"You're too nice," Marta added.

Carmen turned in her seat to face her classmates. "Yeah, she'll come up to us in the hall later and be like, 'Sorry I yelled in class.'"

Suleika looked at me as if I were a child and she the adult. With an expression of patient sympathy she explained, "You don't have a mean bone in your body."

But they did settle down and get to work. I asked them to think about what they wanted to use their voices to say. What would they like to tell the world about their lives? What would they like to tell the governor-elect? Or white people in general? What should the world know about them?

Finally they were writing, shifting in their seats, moving pencils across the page, crumpling disappointing efforts and shuffling papers before starting anew. I made my rounds, checking in with students and seeing who needed help. Once again, Desiree was not writing. "You're breaking my heart," I said. She looked up at me without lifting her head. "I know you have something to say."

She shook her head. Desiree had been in class for a few weeks now, and so far she had not written a word.

"Start by writing the words *I just want to say...*, and see what comes out." She dutifully wrote the words on the page. Then her pencil hovered at the edge of the white expanse and stayed there. "Don't think too much," I said. "Just write the first thing that comes to mind."

I moved on to the next desk, and the next. Then Ruth waved me over. "I memorized it," she said.

"You what?"

"The poem you made us do."

"You memorized the Elizabeth Barrett Browning sonnet?"

Ruth nodded. She pinched her lips together into an almost-smile, her equivalent of beaming.

I tried not to let the utter surprise I was feeling creep onto my face. Ruth had memorized the poem? I had been repeating my challenge to the students for two months now, but as far as I could tell, none had yet made a serious effort to commit those fourteen lines to memory. Finally, I offered a twenty-five-dollar gift certificate to the local mall to anyone who could recite it without a mistake. The certificate had been given to me, and because I rarely shopped at the mall, I decided to use it as bait—or a bribe, as other teachers at the center had called it.

Ruth, who hardly uttered a word during class, who wrote with a penmanship so tentative and small that her words hardly even disrupted the whiteness of the page, was not on my short list of students most likely to take on the challenge.

"You can come to my office at lunch and recite it for me, or you can do it here in front of the class." I was trying to contain my elation.

"The whole class," she said.

"You want to say it to the entire class?" I was surprised again. I didn't expect her to choose this more public option.

Ruth nodded.

When writing time was up, I announced that someone had memorized the poem and, if she could recite it without any mistakes, she might just be the winner of the gift certificate. The girls glanced around, suddenly jealous that they had not bothered to try.

"Ruth," I said, motioning for her to stand. Meanwhile the other students looked on with shocked expressions. *Ruth?* Ruth of the "Whatever" T-shirt? Ruth who clung to the seat in the corner closest to the door as if waiting for the right moment to escape? *Ruth had memorized the poem?* But no one said a word, and in a moment they blinked back any show of caring and reverted to their customary stares of disinterest.

Ruth pushed one palm down on her desk and the other on the back of her chair and lifted her large body by slow increments until she was standing. She took a few steps to the front of the room.

"How do I love thee," she began, hurrying the syllables from her mouth as if they were children she was prodding to cross a busy street. She shifted from foot to foot and stared up over her classmates' heads to the corner where the wall met the ceiling. "I love thee to the breadth and depth and height my soul can reach, when feeling out of sight..."

The poem, as she recited it, lacked all rhythm and grace. The beauty was in the fact that she was saying it at all.

First Kiss[22]

I remember going 45 minutes past my curfew.
Playing curve ball with my homeboy Eddie in
the streets of Paresells.
I remember the smell of his sweet strawberry
lollipop from his breath as the summer breeze
passed us.
Seeing his hazel eyes stare at my brown
eyes and telling me he likes me a lot.
I remember the shine of his red bright shirt
off the sunny sun and hearing the cars
pass us by.
I remember for a minute closing my
eyes to think and in that second I felt the
sweetness of his wet lips against mine.
It felt like I was floating through the
clouds like a bird.
He was as smooth as summer wind
passing by.
And that indeed was my first kiss
with my homeboy Eddie who was as fine
and smooth as Romeo coming to rescue me.

CHAPTER FIVE

BRINGING MRS. TOWNE HOME

WHEN I ARRIVED FOR CLASS ON MONDAY THERE WAS A NEW GIRL sitting in the second row. She was dressed in a cap-sleeved T-shirt with "Hottie" written in silver glitter across her chest. Her cinnamon-colored hair hung loose around her shoulders. "This is Samantha," Latisha said, pointing to the girl, who looked up and smiled.

"Nice to meet you, Samantha," I said. The minute the name was out of my mouth I realized I'd landed in a trap. Latisha had been grinning, which should have been enough to tell me something was wrong. But more important, I'd missed the obvious sign that trouble was underfoot. What Puerto Rican girl is named Samantha, anyway?

A few girls started to giggle, and then the whole class was awash in snickers. Suleika looked up at me with a pained expression. "She's Crystelle," Suleika explained in her patient, tired voice.

That got Latisha laughing even more.

"My name's Tzivia," I said, looking directly at Crystelle, and trying to ignore the swelling wave of laughter. "It might sound like I made that name up, but I didn't." I shot Latisha a warning look. Crystelle nodded, trying, I thought, to impersonate a well-behaved student. But my instinct told me otherwise. Now Latisha had a sidekick.

I wrote some words up on the board that I wanted to review with the class: cliché, imagery, metaphor. But Latisha had gotten to me. I looked up and saw that I'd accidentally written an L instead of an H.

"Metaplor," Latisha sneered. "What's *that*?" She pulled out a tube of bronze lip gloss and began applying it to her mouth. Even as I felt the anger burn beneath my skin, I couldn't help notice how the lip gloss matched Latisha's bronze halter top perfectly.

"You know what it is," Suleika said. "Metaphor. Like comparing."

"Like ... this teacher can't even spell," Latisha spat.

"Listen," I said, "we need a new start in this class. I don't like to make rules the way I would for little kids; you are all adults raising children of your own. But I do need to ask that we respect one another. The bottom line in this class is that if anyone can't treat me—and one another—with respect, I'll have to ask that person to leave." Latisha leaned back in her chair and whispered something to Crystelle.

"Latisha!" I nearly yelled.

"I don't need to listen to this kindergarten shit!" Latisha stood and stomped past me.

"Please don't come back," I told her.

"Don't worry, I won't," she said, and right on cue, slammed the door shut.

Later that day, I was talking to my partner over dinner. When she asked how my day had been, I started to recount the scene with Latisha. I described what had happened, and described my overall frustrations. "I can't believe I threw a student out of class," I said.

"It sounds like she threw herself out."

"Still, I told her not to come back," I said, trying to retain at least a shred of dignity. "I don't know if I even want to go back tomorrow. I mean, if they don't want to learn, why should I want to teach them?"

"I don't blame you for feeling frustrated."

"I'm on the verge of giving up. Tell me I'm overreacting," I said.

"Maybe you're just starting to think about yourself," she offered.

Starting to think about myself? In a strange way, I admitted to myself, I'd been thinking about myself all along. That is to say, while my friends all told me they admired me for taking this job working with underprivileged teens, as if I were some kind of martyr, I knew that on some level my work at the center was more about my love for poetry than for these difficult students. Or maybe I was in love with the *idea* of teaching difficult-to-reach students. I had cast myself as Meryl Streep in *Music of the Heart*, a movie I'd rented on video recently, and which told the story of a violin teacher who hooks a school full of inner-city kids from Harlem on classical music. In my self-scripted movie (call it *Poetry of the Heart?*), I was the Happy Teacher who was patient and positive, no matter what. I was the good citizen who was doing my part. I was, in essence, a fictionalized version of myself. I couldn't seem to admit to myself, let alone my students, that I was fed up. That I was out of control, over my head, out of my league.

I'd made my students into fictions, too. They were the noble poor, hungry for language and culture—my culture, that is.

How many times had I quoted the Pulitzer Prize–winning poet Gwendolyn Brooks to my students: "Poetry is telling my particular truth the way I see it," she'd said during a reading I'd heard her give a few years earlier. But where was the truth in the little drama into which I'd cast my students and myself?

I was glad I wouldn't have to face Latisha the next day. Instead, I met with the students in my autobiography workshop. Discipline wasn't the issue with these students, because everyone in the class had chosen it as one of her electives. My challenge with this group had been finding exercises that would help them tell small, manageable parts of their life stories, so as not to be overwhelmed by the pain.

For this day's writing prompt, I'd chosen the phrase, "Before I was born." I asked the students to write everything they knew or imagined had happened in their parents' lives before their birth. I asked: How did your mother and father meet? Were they in love? What did your mother do before she had babies? How many children were born before you were?

It wasn't one of the prompts I imagined would open the floodgates of emotion. But as was so often the case that winter, I was wrong.

"I hate my parents," Ebony scrawled across the top of her page. "They left me to raise myself for the past six years. No one should ever have to do that. Now their grandchild will be born and they will never meet him." When the front and back of the page was filled with a penmanship that was growing in size in proportion to her rage, she slammed the notebook down in front of me. "I'm done. That's all I have to say."

We were only five minutes into a fifteen-minute free-writing exercise. Normally I would challenge a student who claimed to be finished so quickly and ask her to write more. Ebony had seen me coax enough students in this way to expect me to say, "Is that *really* all you have to say? I suspect there's more inside." Instead I said, "I don't blame you for being angry." Ebony stormed out of the room. I followed her into the hallway and suggested she go and speak with her counselor.

I returned to class. Desiree's page was blank, save for her name written in fastidious script in the top right-hand corner. I looked from her page to her empty eyes. "I don't know anything about my father," she said. This was the most Desiree had said to me in the months I'd been working with her. Slender, and with copper skin, almond eyes, sloping cheeks, and a prim nose, Desiree was, I imagined, the model a Disney animator would choose if he were to draw a Puerto Rican princess.

"Did you ever meet him?"

A nod.

"Is he still alive?"

Another nod. "He left when I was two." I could see the heartbreak glance across her eyes, swift as a kiss. I looked down at her page again and felt overwhelmed. Like white noise that seems to mask sounds with silence, I felt the absence of Desiree's words like the culmination of all of the unvoiced stories I'd heard inside that classroom: Father dead. In jail. Absent. Mother on drugs. Crazy. Abusive. Mother strong. Trying. Battling the odds. Cousin shot. Baby's father cruel. Mother in jail. Baby's father dead. House burned down. Murdered her baby's father. Self-defense. Black eye. Benefits cut. Cousin on drugs. Teacher called her stupid. Little brother almost died. Father cruel. Shelters. Foster homes. Mother gave up custody. Mother gave up. Raised by an aunt. Shot. Robbed. Raped.

"Time's up," I said. As Marta capped her pen, I imagined she capped her pain, as well. In that moment, I wished I could gather up all of the sorrow and strife that had been released into the room, and push it back inside, but like trying to coax a genie back into a bottle, I could see it was impossible. I glanced around the room. Ebony's seat was empty. Desiree had crumpled her paper into a ball. Jazmin sat in her chair immobile, every fiber in her being seemingly focused on not moving, like a small animal on the forest floor who believed that if she stayed perfectly still, danger could not distinguish her from the bark of a tree or the blanket of leaves on the ground.

Esme was shaking out her hand from the effort of writing. I could see the rest of the girls mentally adjusting their expressions, covering emotion with attitude as easily as they put on eyeliner each morning. I needed to find a way to help them navigate feelings that I was just as tempted to hide from as they were.

"Before we read these pieces out loud," I said, "I want everyone to take a moment to imagine someone who makes you feel safe." I paused, anticipating their responses ("No one makes me feel safe," or "My grandma/uncle/father/brother did but she/he is dead/in jail/in Puerto Rico"). "Or," I offered, "if it's not some *one*, imagine some *place* or some *thing* that makes you feel safe. It might be that you feel safe in the bathroom with the door locked or when you are lying in the arms of your lover. It might be you always felt safe with your grandmother and now just remembering her makes you feel taken care of. Whatever it is, try to picture that person, place, or thing in your mind," I said. "Now, I want you to remember that when you are writing in this class, the words on the page can't hurt you." I held up a piece of loose-leaf paper to make my point. "When the things you wrote about happened to you, you were not in charge. But now, when you are writing them down, you *are* in charge. Every time you sit down to write, I want you to remember that."

By the time we were ready to read our stories out loud, there were only five minutes left until the end of class. "We can read these to each other next time," I said. "It's about time to go."

Usually they fled from class and down the stairs before I could even finish saying, "Good work today, ladies." Instead, they slowly pulled themselves out of their seats, collected their pens and backpacks and purses, and left the room. I sat with Jazmin for a few minutes while she smoothed out the crumpled page I'd talked her out of throwing into the trash. I complimented her on her courage in facing the feelings that had come up in her writing. I told her she could talk to me or her counselor about anything she was thinking.

After she left, I walked down to the second-floor kitchen where Celia was heating her lunch in the microwave. "Haven't had a minute all day," she said, nodding toward the clock. It was a quarter to three. Celia was wearing a long, purple, tie-dyed dress and a necklace that reminded me of a string of walnut shells. Her eyelashes looked like rows of exclamation points, but her eyes beneath were always full of sadness. She'd lost her mother when she was very small and had been raised by her father. Her whole being seemed to be a battle between despair and insistent optimism. I remembered something Michelle, the financial officer, had told me one day when we were eating lunch in that room together. Michelle, who always dressed professionally and was meticulous in carrying out her duties, exuded an air of competence. That lunch hour, though, she made some comment about having had a rough time as a teen. I'd assumed she meant she'd smoked a few cigarettes and went too far with a boy at a dance once. But she explained that her problems had been much more complex.

"You?" I said, unable to hide my surprise. "You seem so—*together.*"

She shook her head, "Tzivia, everyone here has something going on. Otherwise they wouldn't be drawn to this place."

I thought of the saying about doctors who can't heal others unless they are in touch with the wounded part of themselves. Maybe the same was true for teachers. To help our students we had to uncover our own wounds. Then I remembered how, two years before, when I'd first signed up to teach in Holyoke, the volunteer coordinator had suggested The Care Center, and when she told me I'd be working with teen mothers, I nearly backed out. What I hadn't said that day was that motherhood was something I didn't always want to think about. I had lost custody of my daughter, and hadn't been able to see or speak to her for five years. In 1988, the year our baby was born, my partner and I had been pioneers in the so-called lesbian baby boom. Before Ellen DeGeneres made being a lesbian acceptable on daytime television and before domestic partnerships were something to be obtained in city halls in some parts of the country and before we ever dreamed we might one day legally marry in our home state, we had become parents together. Then two years later, we broke up. My ex-partner, the baby's biological mother, took our daughter from me. I, having neither the blood ties nor the legal standing a court required, was denied the right to visit her or have contact of any kind. I never mentioned this to anyone at The Care Center. Even now that I had my daughter back, I, the writing teacher, couldn't find the words to express the pain of that particular loss.

I pushed those thoughts aside, as I often did, for fear they would swamp me otherwise. And, as I had also become accustomed to doing, I shifted my focus instead to my work. I began to tell Celia about the class, and Ebony's outburst and Desiree's refusal to write. "I feel like I'm torturing them. I'm asking them to do the most difficult thing, I'm asking them to write about their lives and let the tears flow, but I know the process is emotionally draining."

"You're not torturing them," Celia said. "You're giving them an opportunity."

In that moment I couldn't take in Celia's encouraging words. Instead, I imagined that the next week our writing table would be empty. I would sit alone with my students' stories stacked in front of me. The writers who had released them having fled, and thus with no one to return to, the inked words would fly off the pages like wandering spirits without a physical heart to lodge in. They would spiral through the air, gather into a funneling wind, whoosh across the room and send papers sailing off the desks, overturn jars of pencils and scatter them across the floor.

"What you're doing with them is great," Celia was saying. "I can see that it's helping them. When they come to my office, they bring me the pages they write in your classes and their work becomes a jumping-off point for our sessions."

Or maybe they *will* come back next week, I thought, as my imaginary classroom snapped back to order. And maybe Jazmin will write more about her alcoholic father. Maybe Ebony will admit she's sad and not just angry. It seemed too much to hope that Desiree would fill her page, but maybe she'd tell me something she remembers about being a child.

The next day, most of the students were away on a field trip, so I had intended to spend the quiet afternoon hours planning and reading papers. But I couldn't focus. I decided that, instead, I needed respite from my students' stories—and my own. I would retreat to the History Room at the library. I could catch up on my work later, and no one would even notice my absence, I reasoned.

But Rhonda saw me gathering up my coat and asked where I was going. She had been getting the blow by blow on all my findings about Mrs. Towne, and some of my excitement about my research had rubbed off on her. So, I thought, I could safely confess my plan to play hooky.

"That sounds great," she said, as we walked downstairs. "I'm supposed to be organizing some activities for a couple of girls who couldn't go on the field trip, but I don't have any ideas. Maybe we could come with you?" she asked, raising her eyebrows and cocking her head in my direction.

"So basically, you have nothing planned and you want me to bail you out?" I asked, stepping into the front office.

"You could say it like that," Rhonda said, flashing a sheepish smile.

I agreed, and dialed the library to let Devon, the curator of the city's historical collection, know we'd be coming.

It was a bright afternoon with a flurry of glittering snow drifting from the trees and rooftops. Rhonda's two students were Sonia, whose third baby had just turned five months old, and Crystelle. Sonia told me that she'd just moved into her own apartment on Chestnut Street; in fact, we could see the building across the empty lot to the west. She was glad to have moved out of her parents' apartment, she said, but it was proving difficult to be on her own. For one thing, in order to keep her welfare checks coming, she couldn't let her boyfriend live with her. He couldn't even keep a change of clothes at her place because there were frequent inspections and she didn't want to lose her housing voucher. Also, with three babies, the simple act of leaving the house was difficult. Although she lived within walking distance of The Care Center, she opted to take the school's van each morning because parading all three children to the on-site day care would prove a nearly insurmountable obstacle. The three-block walk we were taking to the library that afternoon represented an unaccustomed flight of freedom for her.

As we approached the library, I opened my tote bag and asked the girls to put the snacks they'd been eating (a bag of Doritos, a bag of sunflower seeds, and a plastic bottle of Pepsi) inside. "Some of the magazines we'll be looking at are nearly a hundred years old," I explained. "We want to be very careful around them."

By now, I'd become such a regular at the long wooden table in the History Room, where I'd sit several times a week surrounded by files of information about Elizabeth Towne and copies of *Nautilus* magazine, that Devon no longer put the materials back where they belonged when I left. Instead, he stacked them on a metal cabinet behind his desk so he could hand them to me when I returned a day or two later. So when we arrived that day, he was ready to greet us with an arm full of file folders and old magazines.

We filled the table I usually occupied alone and divided the papers among us. Rhonda opened a manila file that contained a short, typewritten autobiographical essay by Towne and some crumbling newspaper clips, including Towne's obituary from the local newspaper. The girls each grabbed copies of the *Nautilus* and began flipping through them. They were amused by the price printed on the cover: twenty cents per issue. They liked the deco-style borders that surrounded poems and essays. Inside a 1917 edition, Crystelle found a poem called "Hope."

"Hey," she said. "We wrote poems about hope in your class last week."

Sonia found the word *prophet* in an article and said, "You used this word the other day." It was as if I were being legitimized in their eyes as they saw these ideas in print in Towne's magazine.

The magazine's stated mission was to promote "self-help through self-knowledge." Teasers for the articles read: "I Healed Myself by the Law of Radiation," "Using Your Imaging Power to Promote Healing," and "Hindu Rhythmic Breathing." Inside, headlines were decorated with small pen-and-ink drawings, and typefaces ranged from workaday fonts to serif-heavy, elaborately calligraphed, and gothic-style letters. The articles reflected Towne's interest in metaphysics, psychology, and New Thought, as well as her radical egalitarian politics. *Nautilus* covered everything from telepathy to auras, haunted houses, gardening, and astrology, and also reserved space for commentaries on national and international politics.

Writers who published in the magazine included the poet Ella Wheeler Wilcox (author of the poem "Solitude," which opens with the oft-quoted lines, "Laugh, and the world laughs with you, / Weep, and you weep alone"), Sinclair Lewis, Orison Swett Marden, and Thomas Dreier, among others. Quotes by Ralph Waldo Emerson and poems by Walt Whitman were sprinkled throughout.

Advertisements—for self-filling fountain pens, electric gadgets for reducing bunions, and bottled remedies for hair loss, weight loss, gout, dyspepsia and constipation—as well as notices for New Thought books and pamphlets (including many of Towne's own) filled almost a third of the magazine.

Perhaps the original advice columnist, Towne solicited readers' letters and answered them in print, enthusiastically exhorting on child rearing, marital discord, and even fashion. Sonia turned to a column in which a mother complained of her daughter's unkempt appearance. Towne responded, "Oh, bless your heart, can't you see that it is probably all your own fault!!" She handed the magazine to Rhonda, who continued to read out loud, "You are probably entirely too much of a stickler for neatness and appropriateness in dress, and your daughter has simply gone to the other extreme in an effort to balance *your* extreme." We all laughed, and Crystelle said her mother was the same way.

From article to article, Towne's voice was by turns adamant and intimate. "Express your Self in your work. Satisfy yourself. Not even Jesus the Christ could satisfy others...Cultivate that inner spirit that says, 'Well done,' at every thought and deed that aims to serve..." began an editorial in a 1920 issue.

"Now that's good advice," Rhonda said. She turned to the back of one issue in which Towne laid out her proposal to recycle Navy ships as floating classrooms that would travel the world. "I like this lady," she declared.

I pointed out the poems Towne included in each edition. "We could make a magazine at The Care Center," I said, articulating an idea that had been running through my mind for weeks now. "We could publish our poems and name it after Mrs. Towne's magazine. We could call it *The New Nautilus*, or *Nautilus Two*, or something."

Sonia and Crystelle looked to Rhonda, as if for guidance.

"Yeah," Rhonda said. "We can make it look like these old magazines, with drawings of pillars and scrolls on the cover."

"We could make the cover in art class," Crystelle suggested.

"And charge money—see if people will buy them," Sonia said.

We walked back from the library still talking about our ideas. What, I wondered, would Mrs. Towne think of a tribute such as this?

The next day at lunch, I returned to the library on my own to consider more carefully the idea of modeling a literary magazine after Towne's. This time the History Room was empty. Even Devon had gone on a lunch break, leaving me alone with the magazines. As I opened the first one, a whiff of the hectic essence of the woman who once tirelessly worked to produce it seemed to be released into the air. The rows and rows of print with double columns crammed with stories and advice in 8- or 9-point type were the visual equivalent of the sound of enthusiastic and constant chatter.

"Dearie, lean close and listen," Towne had written in a letter of advice to a reader in 1914. But I felt as if she were speaking to me. I imagined I could feel her breath on my cheek. I could see her, wisps of white hair escaping from the bun set high on the back of her head and forming what appeared to be an aura of charged particles around her. I could imagine Towne wearing a high-collared white blouse, the long sleeves pushed up just above her wrists, and a plain, dark skirt that floated an inch or two above the floor as she marched through her oak-trimmed offices barking commands at stenographers and secretaries.

She ruled her small empire, I learned, from an O-shaped desk in her second-floor office—which, it turned out, was the room where, in my first weeks at the center, I had read, along with my new students, the newspaper article about her life. Towne would sit in the hollow center of that desk, speaking her articles into a Dictaphone for one of the stenographers to type later.

Nautilus was Towne's enchanted world of manageable chaos, fueled by the constant crisis of looming deadlines, and humming with the swish of pencils sweeping over manuscript pages, the staccato of typewriter keys striking paper, and the irregular rush of leather-soled boots on tired wood floors. Most days the bustle of a dozen or more employees sorting mail, addressing magazine wrappers, and proofreading copy would feed her spirits and imbue her with a sense of bubbling contentment. Her voice, goading, prodding, advising and prescribing, would have echoed off the walls where I now encouraged my students to write.

By the time I returned to the center that afternoon, classes had ended and students were pouring down the stairs and out the front door. Some had babies in their arms, and some pulled toddlers by the hand. I walked past as they grabbed car seats from the pile on the porch, and then loaded into the vans to return to their homes.

As I climbed the stairs to my office—the room where, I'd learned in my readings that day, Towne had once hosted meetings of the Hampden County Women's Club (which she founded) and the Holyoke Business and Professional Woman's Club (of which she was president)—the air seemed to be vibrating with intensity, as if the excitement I'd been feeling had stirred every invisible molecule. Or maybe this was the same buzzing urgency that had been vibrating in these rooms for more than a century.

Towne published the first *Nautilus* magazine in Portland, Oregon, in November 1898, which coincidentally was the same year the house at 247 Cabot Street, which would eventually become her home, was built. It was also the year that the United States acquired Puerto Rico as part of the spoils of the Spanish American War, a fact that would have seemed wholly distant to Towne's life at the time, but the repercussions of which would come to her doorstep, literally, a century later.

The way Towne used to tell it, the idea for *Nautilus* came to her in the form of a disembodied voice urging her to become a magazine publisher. It was a story she would recount during interviews, in her memoirs, and in editorials she published in her magazine. Towne may well have been visited by a voice from beyond, but there were other, more prosaic forces at work as well. An earthly inspiration to publish came from her friend Helen Wilmans, publisher of *Freedom* magazine. In 1898, Towne wrote to Wilmans:

> So well has FREEDOM taught and so well have I learned and put in practice the principles of success that here the little *Nautilus* bobs up serenely and maybe a bit saucily alongside FREEDOM, toots her shrill whistle and signals, "Salute me please! but if you won't I shall sail along anyhow!" Success belongs to us both.[23]

The sea image was a fitting one. Towne named her magazine after the poem "The Chambered Nautilus" by Oliver Wendell Holmes. The poet's "venturous bark that flings / On the sweet summer wind its purpled wings" was an apt metaphor for Towne's "saucy" little magazine. In each edition of *Nautilus* Towne included the final stanza of that poem, which reads:

> Build thee more stately mansions, O my soul,
> As the swift seasons roll
> Leave thy low-vaulted past
> Let each new temple nobler than the last
> shut thee from heaven with a dome more vast
> Til thou at last are free
> Leaving thine outgrown shell by life's unresting sea.

The nautilus, celebrated for its ability to grow new chambers to add to its shell, proved a fitting description for Towne's *Nautilus*. The magazine would itself move into new, ever more stately, chambers several times. It progressed from its original home in Portland, where Towne pasted up her magazine at her kitchen table, with her children, Chester and Catherine, then fifteen and seventeen, helping to sort mailing labels and prepare the journals for shipping; to Sioux Falls, South Dakota, where Towne lived for nine months while waiting for her divorce to be finalized; then to two successive apartments in Holyoke when she first arrived and moved in with her second husband, William—and finally to the house on Cabot Street, where *Nautilus* would settle down for good.

The original *Nautilus* consisted of four pages and was printed in the form of a newspaper. The first edition of 4,500 copies cost $36.93 to publish, wrap, and mail.[24] To get started, Towne borrowed $30 a month from her father, and a subscription list of 2,800 names from another self-help magazine.

Small though it was, the early *Nautilus* created a sizable fury. In its first years, the magazine was censored, and Towne was charged with sending obscenity through the mails. In the edition in question, she had written an article in which she argued the benefits of extramarital affairs for traveling businessmen.[25]

She wasn't the only New Thought publisher whose journal drew the attention of censors. At the turn of the nineteenth century, a time when women's career choices were severely limited, it became increasingly common for women to publish small journals and pamphlets as a means of earning an independent income. Many of these journals dealt with topics including family life and relationships. But the idea of women publicly expounding on marital relations, or sex in any context, was considered radical—even immoral. Statutes against sending obscene materials through the mails provided an excuse to quiet these unconventional female voices. Towne's role model, Helen Wilmans, faced obscenity charges for articles she published in *Freedom*, as did several other New Thought authors. One particularly disturbing case caught Towne's attention, and attracted her support.

Ida Craddock, who was born in Philadelphia in 1857, lectured and published articles about female sexuality. She boldly encouraged women to take an active role in sexual intercourse. In one article, she advised newlyweds to enjoy "an hour of tender, gentle, self-restrained coition." In 1902, four years after Towne was cleared of obscenity charges herself, Craddock was arrested for violating New York's anti-obscenity law by sending copies of her pamphlet, "The Wedding Night," through the mails and was sentenced to three months in the city workhouse. After her release, she was arrested again, this time under the federal Comstock law, a statute that was passed in 1873, and which was meant to stamp out indecency. During her ordeal, Craddock wrote to Towne seeking support. Towne replied, in part: "Success is surely yours and my WORD is with you. This is a proptious [sic] time for liberals, according to astrology. And the indictment against Helen Wilmans has been quashed..." Towne's optimism in this case turned out to be unfounded. On October 6, 1902, rather than return to prison, Craddock committed suicide by slashing her wrists and inhaling natural gas.[26]

Towne, meanwhile, pushed forward. By 1905 she employed four stenographers. The next year she moved to Cabot Street, where at any given time she would have a dozen or more stenographers and secretaries working in the first-floor offices. In 1907, seemingly drunk on the taste of her own success, Towne announced that her new goal was to reach one million readers each month. At the time, she had 28,000 subscribers and estimated that she had at least 150,000 readers for each edition, because magazines were assumed to be shared by more than one person. She estimated that in just under a decade, a total of 2.5 million copies had been distributed.[27]

Towne's success was impressive at a time when competition was fierce among New Age periodicals. By 1902 there were over one hundred New Thought publications, with new journals starting up, and others folding each month. At its height, *Nautilus* had a monthly circulation of between 90,000 and 120,000. It became the best-selling New Thought publication of its time. Through her magazine, books, and lectures, Towne's words were said to have influenced more than a million people.[28]

For Towne, publishing and freedom were synonymous. *Nautilus* released her from her unhappy first marriage and financial dependence on a husband who would never treat her as an equal partner. The income earned from publishing allowed her to support herself and her two teenage children and soon led her to her second husband, with whom she would form a productive, equal and loving union of sixty years.

If only, I thought, writing could be as powerful and liberating for the girls who now occupied her house. If only language and self-expression could spark their transformations.

The next week I brought to class a stack of literary journals I'd found in bookstores and on my shelves at home and passed them around the room. I explained that a few of us had come up with the idea of starting our own magazine and began to detail how a journal is made: poets submit their work and editors review the poems received, then a select few are chosen for publication.

"How much do you get paid?" Marta asked.

"There's not much money involved," I said. "Sometimes you just get a copy of the journal."

"That's whack," said Ebony, who had her head on her desk and appeared to be napping.

"The good part is that you get to see your poem in print. You get to tell the world what you think and how you see things."

"I want something in a journal," Marta said. She straightened her spine and cocked her head. "I'll be famous."

I handed out a list of submission guidelines I had typed up and explained that students could submit up to five poems they had written in class for review, but that only one or two would be chosen.

"Starting next month, my afternoon writing class will be devoted to creating the journal. Students in that class will be on the editorial board. We'll select the poems to put in the journal. We'll decide how the cover will look and how the inside pages will look."

After discussing the new magazine, we had twenty minutes left to write. I suggested the students use the time for free writing. "Think with your pens, not your brains." They sat frozen.

"But how do I start?" Evelyn asked.

"Start with the words *I remember*," I suggested, "and see what flows from that. Just write whatever comes to mind."

As I looked around the room, I saw the usual—students writing their names over and over, thinking I'd believe they were writing a masterpiece and leave them alone, students with pens hovering above the page and writing nothing, and students laboriously scratching words onto the page as if they were fulfilling some obligation in a forced labor camp. As usual, Latisha looked angry and bored. Lethal, even. Since the last class, when she'd slammed out of the room, I'd rehearsed all the ways I would dismiss her, ignore her, or lecture her. Instead, I remembered a teacher telling me that the student who gives you the hardest time is the one who needs to be in your class the most. "Stuck for something to write about?" I asked her.

She didn't say anything, but her face seemed to harden even more. She looked, I realized then, like I do when I'm about to shatter into tears. "Just put what's in your mind on the page. No one has to read it if you want to keep it to yourself," I said.

As I began to walk away I heard her mutter, "I write *when* I want, *if* I want."

I continued around the room. Desiree was filling her page with rows of evenly spaced x's and o's. Sylvie was looking ponderously at the ceiling. "No thinking, just write," I said as I walked past. Ruth looked up when I reached her desk. She was barely recognizable. Gone was the "Whatever" T-shirt and in its place was a new red shirt that exposed one ample shoulder. Her hair was elaborately spiraled into a hive from which spilled ribbons of deftly curled tresses. "How do you spell *caress*?" she asked. Behind her, Marta was hard at work, her hand flying across the page. A look of elation spread across her face as she threw words onto her paper.

"I see you're inspired," I said. She nodded without looking up. Marta hadn't produced anything noteworthy in weeks. I usually left students alone when they were concentrating so well, but I couldn't resist. "Are you writing something for the poetry journal?" I ventured.

"Hell, yeah," she answered, eyes still glued to the page. "I wanna see my name in print."

I checked on a few other students, then looked back at Latisha. She might as well have been sculpted from rock. Her skin was flawless, her eyes wide, her nose flat. She'd let the red highlights grow out and now her hair was blacker than black. Her face was full of the meanness that comes of pain—and she was writing.

"I'm glad to see you got inspired today," I said as I stopped to collect her poem at the end of class. The other students were filing out the door on their way to parenting class. Latisha pushed her paper at me. The abrupt gesture was, I knew, an offering of sorts. I took the page and began to read. The title of her poem was, "The Way Life Is."

"See," she said. "I write when I'm ready. I just need time. And everything there is true. There's no BS on that paper."

I tried to let what she had written seep into my skin, to imagine what it would be like to live in those words. "You're a good writer," I said. "How did it feel to put it all down on paper? Any better?" She nodded, and I let myself think I saw something soften in her hard, brown eyes. "I'm glad you did it," I said. "I'm glad it felt okay."

THE WAY LIFE IS[29]

I feel very hurt, tired
and frustrated.

I feel hurt when I get treated unfairly.

I feel tired when I don't
get enough sleep because my
baby is sick.

I feel frustrated when
people in school are all over
my business.

I feel hurt to see that
I'm always sad.

I am tired of feeling like
I can't accomplish my dreams.

I am frustrated when what
I do doesn't satisfy anybody
not even myself.

CHAPTER SIX

I WANT TO WRITE THE POEM

I PULLED UP AT THE CURB IN FRONT OF THE CARE CENTER just as Rhonda was getting out of her car. I parked and caught up with her as she opened the front door to the building, and together we threaded our way through the knot of students in the front hallway.

"So, I did it," I told her. We'd made it into the relative quiet of the office, where we would pick up our mail and memos.

"Did what?" Rhonda asked.

"I wrote a poem," I said. Earlier that week, Rhonda had challenged me to try writing a rap poem, because I'd never done it before, and because I'd asked her to help me teach a workshop on spoken-word, or hip-hop, poetry.

"Let's hear it," Rhonda said again, as she stood shuffling through handfuls of papers: student lists, minutes from a staff meeting, and a memo about an upcoming professional development workshop.

"I'll show it to you when we get upstairs," I said.

"You'll *read* it to me when we get upstairs," Rhonda said. "Remember, you've got to put attitude behind these poems. You can't just let them sit there on the paper and do all the work for you."

As we walked up to our office, I was already regretting my decision to co-teach a spoken-word workshop. I was skeptical of poetry that came with so much emphasis on performance, suspecting that the attention on dramatic delivery served to deflect notice from the inferior quality of the poem itself. Then there was the fact that the poems were usually performed at "slams" and scored based on the instantaneous deliberation of a panel of judges, as if the poem were an ice-skating routine, rather than a soulful expression that might take months or years for a listener to fully digest and appreciate. But Rhonda had convinced me that this might be a form of poetry that would inspire the students.

I closed the door to our office and pulled the poem out of my bag.

"Let's hear it," Rhonda said. She leaned into the crackling vinyl cushion of her desk chair and flashed an expectant smile my way. I stood before her like a sixth-grader alone on a stage during a spelling bee and began to read. When I was finished she whooped and clapped the way she would for one of our students who'd managed to put together a half-intelligible paragraph for a writing assignment. "Not bad for a white girl," she said.

"Gee, thanks." I stuffed the poem back into my bag. "I'm just glad you'll be doing most of the teaching in this workshop, not me."

"We'll see," Rhonda said.

Just then Carmen burst into the room and dropped into the chair next to Rhonda's desk.

"Hey, Rhonda! Look what I got," she said, pushing a large white envelope into Rhonda's hands. Inside were studio portraits of her daughter, who was posed with a Santa's hat perched on her black curls. In her lap she held an oversize present elaborately wrapped in shiny green paper. Rhonda began exclaiming over the baby's eyes and nose, commenting on which features were Carmen's and which were from the baby's father.

Somehow I felt that I was the one who had interrupted a conversation. "I've gotta go teach," I told Rhonda, as she continued to ooh and aah over Carmen's pictures.

When I entered the classroom, Desiree, who was usually so quiet, was announcing that she had watched President Bush on television the night before. I was used to entering a classroom and hearing students holding forth on each other's hairstyles, boyfriends, or plans to go clubbing. Given the content of this morning's discussion, rather than try to quiet them as I normally would, I took a seat and began to unpack papers, folders, and books from my tote bag, while taking in the girls' conversation. "I can't believe he's going to make us go to war. I don't want to be in no war," one girl was saying.

I organized my piles of lined paper for writing and the photocopied poems for the day's lesson. I'd brought in a poem by Alix Olson, a
spoken-word poet whose work I'd found in an anthology of rap poetry
that Rhonda had loaned me, and who had written a mercifully unsen-
timental rap about her daughter. I was hoping it would spark some
original writing about motherhood, instead of what I usually got from
my students, about how their babies were "little angels sent from
heaven." But I was beginning to doubt we'd get to the poem at all that
day.

Now Suleika was putting in her two cents about the president:
"All those white people voted for him and put him in office, and now
look," she said. There was a lull in the conversation, as if my presence
had suddenly registered. "No offense," Suleika said, looking my way.

I was the only representative of "all those white people" in the
room, and twelve pairs of eyes were on me.

"Don't look at me; I didn't vote for Bush," I said.

Ebony couldn't hide her surprise, or her disbelief. "You did, too,"
she said. "All white people voted for Bush."

"Really, I didn't," I said. I couldn't believe I was in the position of
having to defend myself against charges of voting for a Republican
president who was keen on war and pleasing members of the Radical
Right. When I was Ebony's age, I'd marched in demonstrations against
nuclear power and nuclear weapons; I'd crisscrossed the country on a
Greyhound bus and joined women's peace encampments.

"You didn't, for real?" Gloria asked.

"You voted for Gore, then?" someone else asked skeptically.

"I voted for Gore. For real," I said, counting out copies of the poem
I was preparing to hand out.

"But all rich white people vote for Bush," Ebony insisted.

Now, not only was I a Republican in their eyes, but I was rich, too.
And not only that, all white people were rich and Republicans.

"It's true that a lot of Republicans are rich and a lot of Republicans are white," I told them. "That's because Republicans tend to want
to protect wealth, and people who have wealth tend to want to protect
it. Still," I added, "not all rich white people vote Republican, not all
white people are rich, and..."

Ebony interrupted me again. "I wanted Bush to win at first," she
said.

"You did?" Now it was my turn to be shocked.

"He looked so old, I felt sorry for him."

"Did you vote?" I asked, knowing perfectly well what her answer would be. She hadn't, and for once I thought that was a good thing.

After class I returned to my office, where Rhonda was reviewing signup sheets for the spoken-word workshop to see who had chosen our class. I told her about the discussion that had taken place downstairs, and how shocked I was that the girls were shocked that I didn't vote for Bush. "The gulf between us is so wide," I said. There was a note of desperation in my voice I hadn't intended to reveal. "They'll never really see me," I said. "My color and my culture will always be in the way."

"You know, Tzivia, when I was their age I thought the same kinds of things," Rhonda said. "I thought white people were this way or that way. I thought they were rich. I thought they were different. I remember the first white person I really saw for who she was. She was my teacher in sixth grade. She was the type of teacher who did things different. She would reveal things to us about herself. That helped us see her as a human being."

We talked for a little while longer. Finally, Rhonda said, "Tzivia, you take everything so seriously. Stop worrying about it."

At lunchtime I usually sat in the staff kitchen on the second floor, rather than eat with the students downstairs, the way most staff members did. I told myself that I liked the quiet of the upstairs kitchen. I usually brought my own lunch anyway, rather than eat the cheeseburgers, fries, pizza, and chicken nuggets that were typically served to the girls. But today I decided to venture downstairs. I was thinking about what Rhonda had said, about teachers who revealed more of themselves making a difference. Maybe I had to be willing to be a little more accessible to my students if I was to understand them, and they me.

I sat at a round table with three other students who paused in their conversation just long enough to notice I'd joined them. I put my insulated lunch bag down in front of me and began to unpack a sandwich bag filled with miniature carrots and a plastic container filled with two salmon cakes and brown rice that were left over from the previous night's dinner. I put the salmon cakes and rice in the microwave to cook, then returned to the table and opened my bag of carrots and began to eat.

"What are you eating?" asked Sylvie, who was seated next to me. Sylvie's horrified question attracted the attention of the others at the table, and the students at the next table over. Soon everyone in the lunchroom, it seemed, was looking in my direction.

I held up a carrot. "Carrots," I said.

"Whole carrots?" she asked.

"Well, they're little carrots," I said. "Don't you like carrots?"

"Carrots cut up, carrots cooked, but not just carrots out of a bag!" Ebony interrupted. She looked to her friends for support. "Look at her eat *carrots!*" she said, as if I were eating raw fish heads, or live frogs.

I tried to explain that carrots are healthful and held out the bag and asked if anyone would like to try one. One or two staff members took one to show that eating raw carrots was not life threatening and that the little orange vegetables wouldn't make them turn white or vote for George Bush.

Still, when the timer chimed on the microwave letting me know my salmon cakes were ready, I gathered up my things and carried my plate back upstairs.

At one o'clock I found Rhonda and we went to the third-floor classroom to teach our workshop. We started off by having the students write a poem as a group. We called it "I Want to Write the Poem," and each student contributed a line that expressed something she'd like to tell the world about her life: "I'd like to write the poem that shows the world all my pain/ I'd like to write the poem that shows my love for my children ..."

After a half hour we had two pages of lines, in English and Spanish, expressing anger, hope, frustration, and determination. After we read what we had out loud, Rhonda did something that wasn't part of our plan.

"Tzivia has written a rap and she's going to read it to us as an example of how we can turn all of these lines into a complete poem."

She turned to me and smiled so hard, I knew she was holding back a laugh and a finger poke, and the taunt, "Gotcha!"

I was going to complain and say no, but I thought again of what Rhonda had said earlier about the value of exposing a little bit of myself to the students. My first effort that day had failed, but here was a chance to try again. I sank my hand into my tote bag. "Okay," I said. "I'll read it if I brought it with me."

"While you're looking," Rhonda said, now in full mischief mode, "I'll get Aimee and Irma so they can listen, too."

Aimee and Irma? Why invite more teachers into the room? I could feel sweat leap from every pore. Even as I located the poem among the papers in my bag, I considered saying I couldn't find it, sorry, maybe next week—but just then Rhonda burst into the room with the two teachers—and Anne, the director of the center.

Rhonda took a seat up front with her arms crossed over her chest. "We're all ready for you now," she said.

I shot her a look that must have been similar to the looks Latisha so often shot me. Then I took my place at the front of the room. "Let's review our rules for listening with respect to each other's poetry," I said.

"Positive feedback," Gloria called out.

"Right. And what else?"

"Active listening," Suleika added.

"We know the rules. You just don't want to read," Sylvie said.

"Come on, you make us do it all the time," Carmen added.

"Right," I said. I looked down at the first line of my penciled composition.

"Go on," Rhonda whispered.

If I hesitated any longer I'd never be able to get the girls to read their work for me again. So I read the title: "I Wanna Write the Poem." I saw Suleika nod and smile. I couldn't help but think she was imitating the silent message of encouragement I used each time a student screwed up her courage to begin to read her poem. Suleika's smile launched me.

"I wanna write a poem that's ghetto, that's black." I could hear some shuffling of papers, girls readjusting themselves in their seats. "A poem that the girls won't say is whack." Someone giggled. "But I'll never write a poem like that./ My poem will be white like the sands of Long Island./ It'll be about a Jewish Princess and her rebellion." I began to read fast, as if in a panic. I *was* in a panic. I told myself what I'd told the girls countless times before: breathe. When I did slow down enough to inhale, I realized I had the girls' attention. I exhaled and read, "I know my poems aren't in fashion," and I caught Rhonda beaming my way. I slowed my voice down and delivered the last stanza louder and with feeling:

> I'm too old to rap
> too young to give up
> No I can't weave words like *phat, chill,* and *wazzup.*
> Listen to me anyway
> Digest the words then let me hear you say:
> I'll write my own
> Declare my voice's poem.
> Hang up that cell phone!
> Turn off the TV
> Put down that blunt.
> Tell me who you want to be.

When I stopped, the students and teachers burst into applause. I saw Sylvie nudge Carmen and say, "Did you hear her say blunt? And whack?"

Marta called out, "That was ghetto fabulous!"

Rhonda looked at me with a smug smile of accomplishment.

"Can I read now?" Ebony asked. She wanted to read our group poem out loud for the guests who'd come into the classroom. Then there was a flurry of requests from girls who wanted to read poems they'd written that morning or in previous classes. Finally it was two-thirty, and time for the students to go home.

—

I sat at my computer drafting a memo to staff about the student journal I planned to launch. I composed a few paragraphs explaining who Elizabeth Towne was, and why we were naming our magazine after hers. But as I cobbled sentences together, I was once more frustrated with how little I knew about Towne. Holyoke's silence on the topic of Mrs. Towne roared in my ears. It felt like a betrayal. After all, this was the same city that memorialized the founding of the game of volleyball with a Hall of Fame in the center of its downtown, a sprawling building dedicated to a minor sport. Shouldn't the fact that Holyoke had been home to one of the foremothers of New Age thinking, a publisher and suffragist, be something worthy of at least a plaque on the front of a house?

Then there was the city's seeming neglect of its immigrant daughters, my students, which I saw as yet another abnegation. Maybe that was what Towne and my students had in common most of all: the silence that threatened to swallow their stories. My plan to start a new *Nautilus* would be, I hoped, a step toward using poetry to right both wrongs.

But if I were to bring Towne back to life in the imagination of her former city, I needed more than the skeletal stories I'd uncovered in the library. I wanted to talk to someone who had known her, someone who carried her story not in the pages of an article or book—but in her blood, in her heart.

I soon became distracted. I clicked onto the Internet and began mousing between search engines: Google, Alta Vista, Lycos, and Jeeves. I wanted to find one of Mrs. Towne's relatives: a great-granddaughter or a great-grand-nephew ... someone who could tell me what she had said, what her voice sounded like, what her handwriting looked like. Someone who had a portrait handed down by her mother's mother, or had a letter that had been saved, or the family Bible, where maybe Mrs. Towne might have recorded birth dates and weddings.

Maybe I wanted her blessing, as I prepared to launch a new magazine in her home. Maybe I wanted to be sure she would have approved, that the spirit that still roamed the house would be consoled—and not offended—by our efforts.

I visited one genealogy website after another searching for the family trees of people with the last name Towne. But that name, not surprisingly, turned up endless pages of hits, and I feared I'd never sort through all of them. I decided to work on Struble, the name of Towne's first husband and the name her son, Chester, carried as well. I soon began coming across the names of familiar characters: Chester. Catherine. Elizabeth Struble Towne. Having landed on the right branch of the family tree, I followed it back to Elizabeth Towne's father, John Halsey Jones, one of Oregon's earliest settlers, who crossed the country from New York to Oregon on a prairie schooner, and who supported his family with his successful lumber mill. There, too, was Towne's mother, Jane Osbourne Jones, a schoolteacher from upstate

New York who followed her husband across the country, and died of yellow fever when Elizabeth was just nine years old.

Then I traced the line forward, until I found the names Paul Froiland Twing and Garrison Struble Twing Jr., both of whom were listed with birth years, but no death dates. These were Elizabeth's great-grandsons, the grandchildren of her daughter, Catherine.

I switched to the online White Pages and by five o'clock I had an email address for Paul and a phone number for Garrison. Without hesitation I tapped out a message to Paul, asking if he'd be willing to talk to me. I pressed "send" and waited. But "waiting," with connotations of passively passing time, was not the right word for what I was doing. I checked my email incessantly, looking for a response. When two hours passed, and I had no reply, I began to worry that I had somehow offended Paul with the wording of my email. Maybe I should have spent more time composing my message, rather than sending it so impulsively. Soon, not only was I checking my inbox, but I was also checking the status of the message I had sent to Paul, who, like me, subscribed to AOL. "Unread," the status window announced. By the next afternoon at three, the status had not changed.

I had hoped to contact Paul through email, rather than using the phone number I'd found to call Garrison. A written inquiry seemed more polite than a phone call from a stranger; especially from a stranger who was not even interested in the recipient himself, but in his distant relative. Still, my excitement about the possibility of being in touch with a living relative of Elizabeth Towne wouldn't let me procrastinate any longer. After work I dialed Garrison's phone number. As soon as he answered I launched into a hasty introduction of myself and my mission.

"Just a minute, I have a cat crawling on my lap," he said. When he settled back into our conversation, his cat presumably curled up on some other chair or in front of the stove, he said, "Yes, I know a little bit about my great-grandmother. She published a magazine; I think it was about women's rights."

I told him that indeed Elizabeth Towne had been a suffragist, but the magazine was mostly about New Thought.

"I think she was the first mayor of Holyoke," he offered. I told him that she *had* run for mayor, but that she lost. I was beginning to despair that I would learn nothing new from this man. "She did become Holyoke's first female city council member, though," I told him, feeling awkward that I seemed to know more about his relation than he did.

"Well," he said, "here's something *I* can tell *you*." My pen was poised, ready for some new tidbit of information. "She was the first woman in Massachusetts to get a divorce," he said.

"Really?" I knew, of course, that she had divorced her first husband, but that was in Oregon, not Massachusetts. Maybe she had also divorced William late in life and that explained why he never visited her in the nursing home. But the first divorce in Massachusetts? That couldn't be.

"Yes," said Garrison. "She ran off with the carriage boy and headed west to Oregon. And she left a good number of little Twings along the Oregon Trail," he boasted.

I put my pen down. This was obviously untrue. For starters, Elizabeth Towne wasn't a Twing; Twing was the name of the man her daughter Catherine had married. And besides, Towne had migrated east, not west. I tried to gently break this news to Garrison.

"Maybe I got that one backwards," he said. "But if it's a good story you're looking for, I could tell you about the Twing side," he offered, and launched into a tale about one of his ancestors who was tortured, then hung and drawn and quartered. "He was a Frog who tried to convert England to Catholicism," Garrison said. "I have some papers here about that side of the family. I can send you copies if you like."

In an effort to steer the conversation back to Mrs. Towne, I asked if he'd ever been to the house on Cabot Street.

"That crazy old place? Sure, I was there fifty years ago. It was jam-packed with stacks of her old magazines. There was hardly room to crawl between the piles," he said.

"Did you take some copies for yourself?" I asked.

"What would I want with all that..." He paused, seeming to be looking for just the right word to carry his disgust. "All that *woman* stuff?" he finally blurted.

I didn't know how to respond. Of all the possible reactions I might have imagined from one of Towne's relatives, somehow I hadn't conjured this one. "Look, if you want to find out more you should talk to

my Aunt Betsy," he said. "She's the family historian. She could probably tell you some stories." He promised to try and find Aunt Betsy's
phone number for me. Then, just before hanging up he asked, "Why
are you doing this?"

He could have meant a hundred different things with that question. He might have wondered if I was an historian or just another
crazy woman's libber like his great-grandmother. Maybe he wondered
if I hoped to make money from Towne's story, or if I was looking for
skeletons in his family's closet.

I don't remember how I answered him that evening, only that after I hung up the phone, his question hung in the air. Why *was* I doing
this? If he had no interest in his great-grandmother, why did I? I had
started all of this just to find out a little bit about the house on Cabot
Street where I was teaching. Then I wanted to find out more about the
woman who had occupied the rooms that my students and I worked
in. Or was it because Mrs. Towne, a teen mother and an independent
woman, seemed so similar to my students? Or because she seemed so
similar to me? Why was I persisting? Hadn't I learned enough already?
Now that I'd gone this far, where would my research end?

Garrison certainly didn't see Towne as a daring, freethinking writer
who broke ground for women in politics, publishing, and religion.
According to him, what I had perceived as Towne's revolutionary spirit
was nothing more than a sorry punch line to an unbalanced story.
Where I saw a principled life and a reasoned feminist analysis, Garrison saw hysterical nonsense.

It was time for dinner. My daughter was at her ballet class and my
partner had gone to an antiques auction, so I was on my own. I took
out a box of pasta and a jar of sauce. As I put the water on to boil, I felt
a wave of despondency wash over me. First Holyoke forgot Elizabeth
Towne, then her own family did. She'd lived boldly and with optimism and faith in the future, only to be written off as one more eccen-
tric old lady, even by her own kin. As I poured the pasta into the pot,
the phone rang.

It was Betsy Twing Bruning, Garrison's aunt. Betsy's voice sounded
as though it were draped in doilies and drenched in peppermint. I
turned off the stove and sat down again at the dining room table.

Betsy was calling from just outside of Milwaukee, Wisconsin, where she'd been living for more than four decades. She told me she was Catherine and Edward L. Twing's daughter, and the "youngest by far" of the Twing and Struble cousins. That would make her Elizabeth Towne's only living grandchild.

"What can I do for you?" she asked, and I felt somehow that she would be pleased to do anything she could.

"Did you meet your grandmother?" I asked.

"Yes, of course. She was at my wedding," Betsy said.

I asked if she had any of her grandmother's diaries, letters, or albums. Did she have any photographs?

Betsy told me she had been an amateur artist and wished she'd had a good photograph of Elizabeth from which to paint a portrait, but one of Chester's grandsons, John Tufts, inherited all of that, she told me. "He had the pictures, the diaries, the letters. We lost touch a long, long time ago. I did ask him to send me some of Grandmother's things, I even sent him the money for postage, but he never did. Now I have no idea where he lives. I don't even know if he's dead or alive."

John Tufts: if I typed that name into Google I'd get a hundred pages of responses, and would have no way of knowing which of all of the John Tufts in the United States was *the* John Tufts. Why couldn't he have had a more original name? I lamented.

"I only know two stories about grandmother," Betsy was saying. The first one involved the fact that Elizabeth was notorious for taking a two-hour nap before lunch every afternoon. "She lay down on the couch in the living room and pulled a paisley shawl over her," Betsy said. The habit was so ingrained that when Elizabeth Towne went to the 1938 World's Fair and naptime came around, she lay down on a bench and closed her eyes. The story goes that two Russian guards watched over her while she slept. "I don't even know if it's true," Betsy said, in a tone that let me know that she cherished the tale, true or not.

Next she told me that her grandmother could not be presented in court in England because of her divorce, but she was invited to a garden party at Buckingham Palace, nonetheless. "She reached out and touched the queen's dress and said, 'What a lovely fabric.'" Betsy added, "I don't know if she knew she shouldn't have touched the dress or not."

Just then Betsy said she had to hang up; someone was knocking on her window. She gave me her phone number and I told her I'd call back.

I rushed through dinner while I waited for enough time to elapse before dialing Betsy's number. I was worried that despite her warm voice, Betsy had concocted the story of the visitor to get me off the phone. After all, what was that about someone knocking on the window? Don't they have doors in Wisconsin?

Finally, I couldn't wait any longer. If she didn't want to speak to me, Betsy could just let the phone ring, or invent another friend who was knocking on the ceiling, this time. So I dialed the number I'd scribbled into my notebook. "I don't want to keep you, but I would like to ask you a few more questions," I said.

"No, not at all," she said, cutting off my apologies. I had the sense that she was settling into a comfortable chair for a long chat. "So, where were we?" she asked, and we continued to talk for over an hour. I told her about what was happening in her grandmother's house now, and she moved from room to room in her imagination trying to remember what each had been used for back then. She told me how her grandmother had been stern and exacting ("She wasn't your cookie-baking kind of grandmother,") and how the family would gather in the house on Cabot Street for Sunday dinners. Betsy tried to help me fill in names on her family tree, and encouraged me to keep trying to find out more if I could.

After I hung up I was elated at having found Mrs. Towne's last remaining grandchild. But, I realized, I'd never even mentioned the new magazine we were about to start. Next time, I thought, and began scribbling down questions I might ask when I called Betsy again.

After that, Betsy and I spoke many times. I would come home to a message from her, or I'd pick up the phone to ask her the questions I'd been saving since our last call. I even began an email correspondence with her daughter, who signed her messages "Tink." She was interested in her great-grandmother's story, but didn't have many facts to share. She did, however, have an unusual strategy she thought might help me find Elizabeth Towne's letters, diaries, and other papers. Towne's husband William, Tink explained in one of her emails to me, now exists as a friendly spirit who continues to roam the halls of The Care Center. She and her husband had visited the building once on a trip east, and they were sure they sensed his ghost. Dick, her husband, had for years been trying to track down the papers in hopes of one day writing a biography of Elizabeth Towne. He had pleaded with William Towne's ghost, telling it that the only way Elizabeth's biography could be written was with his cooperation, but so far there had been no offers of heavenly aid.

"Dick suggests lovingly touching the walls of (William's) room and talking to Great-Grandfather," Tink wrote me in one email.

The next time I spoke to Betsy, I mentioned her daughter's suggestion. Betsy agreed wholeheartedly that conversing with Grandfather Towne's ghost would be an excellent idea. I was sitting on my bed holding the phone to my ear with one shoulder, while I took notes on our conversation on a pad I'd propped on my knees. I didn't want to offend Betsy by suggesting this idea was ludicrous; after all, Elizabeth Towne herself would likely have approved of such a plan. Betsy explained that, unfortunately, she couldn't negotiate effectively with spirits, but that I might be more successful. "I don't have the gift, but others have seen Grandmother. They say that when she appears she comes surrounded by a whole *entourage*."

I asked Betsy to tell me more about her own mother, and how Catherine and Elizabeth got along. As we were talking, the ceiling light in my room began to flicker on and off. Perhaps this electrical irregularity was a sign that Elizabeth was listening in on our conversation, and that she approved of the idea of talking to walls, I thought, letting myself get carried away by Betsy and Tink's otherworldly suggestion. My heart began to race as I let myself become convinced that pleading with William from within his office, if only I knew which room it was, would lead me directly to Elizabeth's papers.

After I hung up the phone, I had to admit to myself that the bedroom light had flickered many times in the past. In fact, the reason I usually used the floor lamp instead of the ceiling light was that I was afraid a mouse or a squirrel had chewed a wire someplace in the attic and that I should have it checked before an exposed wire caused a fire that would destroy my house, and with it all the notes I'd been collecting about Elizabeth Towne.

But logic had less firm a hold on me than did the allure of a good ghost story. The next day I arrived at The Care Center a little early,

hoping to find William's office so I could talk to the walls before everyone else arrived. Referring to Tink's email, I tried to make sense of
her description of where William's room was located.

"I recall that it was a sunny room—maybe a corner room down
the hall from the stairs???" she'd written. There were two staircases
that led to the second floor hallway, and at least six rooms that could,
based on the rambling architecture of the house, be considered corner
rooms. Depending on the time of day, almost all could be considered
sunny, as Towne, who believed in the curative powers of sunshine,
made sure her house contained multiple large windows in every room,
and covered none of them with shades or curtains. But I had another
piece of information, too. Betsy had told me that there would be a cat
port on the door to William's office. He was so devoted to his cats that
he had porches built for them outside the windows on the second story.
This explained why those porches had long since been sealed from
use; they had been built to hold the weight of sunning cats—not people.

I walked through the halls, stopping in front of each door and looking for signs that there had once been a missing panel close to the
floor where a cat port might have been attached. I was squatting before the closed door to a likely office, running my fingers over the dry
wood of the lower panel, when suddenly, the door swung open. Startled,
I looked up to see Selenia, one of the counselors on staff, standing
above me. She was neither smiling nor frowning, simply gazing down
at me. She wore a sensible outfit of loose-fitting slacks and a comfortable tunic. With her graying hair coiled into tight curls and wire-
rimmed glasses slipping down her nose, she looked stern and gentle,
the way I imagine grandmothers should. "Can I help you with something?" she asked, as if I had politely knocked on her door.

I stood, trying desperately to think of some reasonable explanation for having been squatting in the hallway, but when none came to
mind, I went with the truth. "I've been reading about the lady who
used to live in this house, and I learned that her husband had a cat and
that he had a cat port on the door to his office," I said.

"You want to see it?" Selenia asked. "It's right here." She pointed
directly across the hall to Celia's office. Celia's door was covered top
to bottom with posters. Selenia leaned over and loosened a thumbtack
holding the corner of a brightly colored poster that proclaimed "Girls

Rule." She peeled the poster back, and there it was: a small, hinged door with a sliding bolt holding it closed.

Just then Celia arrived. She paused and asked us what we were doing. "Oh, she wanted to see the cat door," Selenia said, and returned to her own office.

Celia pushed past me into her room and lowered her overstuffed shoulder bag and an armload of papers onto an empty chair. She was wearing a flowing cotton dress and so much silver jewelry that when she moved she sounded like excited nerves—or a carnival wagon.

I told her what Tink and Betsy had told me about the building being haunted by William's spirit. "I always assumed it was the lady's spirit," Celia said. "But either way, I think it *is* haunted. For starters, the thing about the cat is really strange," she said as I took a seat alongside her desk. She reminded me about the cat that used to crawl into the former GED teacher's first-floor classroom, and the other cat that would sit at the front door until someone had pity on him and let him in. Still another cat had recently given birth to a litter of kittens in the basement, she said. Maybe there is a spirit in the house that attracts them, she suggested. "In the summer, this office still smells of cat piss. The smell just won't go away. I always keep my door closed when I'm not here, so I know there hasn't been a cat in here for years."

It would have been more than forty years since William's cat could have had any accidents that would have caused the office to smell. Of course, there might have been a more recent feline tenant, because the building had been used first by a family, then by a variety of social service agencies, in the years since the Townes passed on.

"You know what else is strange?" Celia said, leaning into a conspiratorial whisper. "See this plant? The soil is always growing mold right on the surface. I can't explain why."

I wasn't convinced that either of these were signs that William's ghost inhabited her office, but I was willing to entertain the possibility. Besides, I'd told Betsy I'd ask the walls for help, and if nothing else seemed to be a sign that this was the right plan of action, the fact that Celia, of all people, would be inhabiting William's office seemed a good omen. I could think of no other staff member who would be so accepting of—even enthusiastic about—having me stand in her office, touch the walls, and plead with an invisible spirit for assistance with a research project. I explained what I intended to do, and Celia stood with me.

"Okay if I talk to him, too?" she asked.

"Of course," I answered, as I put my hand on the wall next to the windowsill where the moldy plant was growing. "William, if you can hear me, I'd really appreciate your help finding Elizabeth's and your papers so I can learn more about all of the good work you both did here." I rolled my eyes in Celia's direction and smiled.

Then she put her hand on the wall. "And William, could you stop playing around with my plants? I don't like that mold stuff," Celia added.

There was a knock at the door and, without hesitation, Celia called, "Come in." I felt like a teenager who was about to be caught smoking in my bedroom. Luz swung into the office, then stopped abruptly as she took in the sight of Celia and me standing, each with one hand on the wall. I dropped mine into my pocket, but Celia didn't budge.

"Come on in," Celia repeated, even though Luz was already standing in front of us. "We were just talking to the walls," she said, matter-of-factly.

"I heard this room is haunted, and we were talking to the spirit," I said, deciding Celia's approach of full disclosure was the best, after all.

Luz's eyes grew wide and she shook her head.

"Don't worry," Celia said, motioning for Luz to sit. "He's a nice ghost."

My Eyes[30]

I was born with eyes of Saturn
They're dark with light rings
for my happiness.
These eyes have seen things
I'll never forget, sights of violence,
sadness, hurt and loneliness. They've
seen pain and discouragement.

Even though my eyes look beautiful
no one can stand to see what
these eyes have seen.

CHAPTER SEVEN

ONE GOOD THING

In class that week we read "Preludes" by T.S. Eliot and "Young Woman at a Window" by William Carlos Williams. We talked about how rather than merely telling the reader how to feel, the author of each poem used descriptions of things (a gusty wind, evening, a mother gazing out a window) to evoke mood and emotion. When it came time to read, Solmary, who was generally quiet and often absent, wrote:

> Through my mom's window I see
> a building on fire
> Through my mom's window I can
> almost smell what the building is going
> through
> Through my mom's window I feel
> my eyes burning like that building
> Through my mom's window I see
> that building fallen and I am
> fallen for that building is my
>   home.[31]

"That was your building?" Sylvie asked. Solmary nodded. We'd all read the newspaper story about the fire that destroyed an apartment downtown earlier that week. Although the days when landlords in Holyoke were said to be regularly torching apartment buildings for the insurance money had been over for decades, Holyoke still seemed to have a disproportionate number of suspicious fires.

Everyone was silent for Solmary's loss. "The poem was phat, though," Latisha said so quietly that it was almost as though she were speaking to herself.

I agreed with Latisha. I was haunted by the lines: "That building fallen and I am / fallen." At first I wanted to suggest she change fallen to falling, suspecting that was what Solmary had meant to say. But fallen made the act one of completed collapse. The sense of the brick and dust surrendering to tragedy, and the poet's surrender to grief, was utterly beautiful. It was a collapse that I felt was threatening my students' will to learn, and my resolve to remain hopeful and detached in the face of their lives.

The school had begun to feel like a revolving door, with students coming and going. Ruth had left after turning twenty-two and "aging out." I hadn't seen Desiree or Ebony for weeks and new students had appeared to take their places.

But that same day, Rhonda brought me the good news I needed. Marta passed the GED, she told me. Finally. I was relieved, especially because the last time Marta had come into the office to tell Rhonda her woes, it sounded like she didn't know how she'd hold on any longer.

Marta had been in and out of our program for more than two years. Her daughter would be entering kindergarten in the fall and her caseworker had warned that her benefits might be cut, as Marta had far exceeded the time limits imposed by welfare reform. Meanwhile, she was hiding from her worker the fact that her eighty-year-old grandfather shared her one-bedroom apartment, sleeping on the living room sofa, and in exchange shared his Social Security checks with her.

Just the week before, on a cold, rainy January afternoon, she'd left the center and headed home on foot. That morning, in an effort to save a few pennies on gas, she'd left her ten-year-old Ford Escort, which she referred to as "the bucket" (short for shit-bucket, she'd once told me), parked on the street outside her building. The car was missing its passenger-side rear window, which she'd replaced with a sheet of plastic and a generous supply of silver duct tape, and the heater didn't work. So in addition to saving gas, walking would keep her warmer than sitting and waiting for the car's engine to warm up during the short drive to the center, she reasoned.

Her daughter was still at preschool and her grandfather was making his rounds downtown, calling on his old friends as he did each day, so Marta thought she would have a little time alone. She climbed three flights to her apartment, which was so small that on opening the door she could see every room at once. Instantly, she knew something was wrong. The cramped living room, which she was always careful to keep tidy, was trashed. Papers and DVDs were strewn across the floor, there were bare spots on the wall where framed pictures had hung, and her DVD player was gone. She had been robbed. Now she cursed the fact that she had walked. If she'd taken the car, she'd have taken her purse, which held her wallet, car keys, and a few twenties that her sister had given her to pay the car insurance bill. Now she noticed the purse was gone, too. She broke down and cried.

At twenty-one, Marta was more used to things going wrong than to having them go right. After three years struggling to pass the GED, she had recently retaken the test and was waiting to find out whether she had failed again. Surveying the extent of her loss after the break-in, she cried out, "I work so hard, why would they take everything?" Then she pleaded with God. "Please," she begged, "let one good thing happen."

Marta told Rhonda this story as she sat in our office and I couldn't help but listen. When she finished, I blurted out, "You should write that down."

"Nah, I don't have the patience for that," she said. "And I'm not a good writer either."

"But you're so articulate," I said. Marta not only had an impressive vocabulary, but she also had a deep, rolling voice punctuated by a confident laugh that made her stories easy to listen to.

"If you want to see my story on paper, you write it down," Marta said.

"Okay," I said. "I'm done teaching today. Make yourself comfortable." I pulled out a notebook and Rhonda said she had to go supervise a prenatal yoga class.

I began asking Marta questions and she answered without hesitation. Her confidence in herself made it easier for me to pry. But after about twenty minutes she said she had to go and pick up her daughter. "You can come by tonight. I'll make you dinner and you can finish your questions," Marta offered.

Driving downtown that evening, I passed City Hall, whose steeple I could see from my office window at the center. Up close it was a looming stone edifice that looked like a cathedral, with stained glass windows and an imposing spire. Just behind City Hall was Heritage State Park, with its antique, dollar-a-ride merry-go-round. On the southern border of the park, before the city deteriorated into blocks of abandoned factory buildings and housing projects, stood the Volleyball Hall of Fame.

As I turned down High Street, I passed "La Favorita Market" and a clothing store whose sign boasted, "South Bronx Fashion." The majority of the city's white residents avoided going beyond this street. It was easy to see why: the neighborhoods south of High Street resembled the set of a disaster movie about a city that has been ravaged by some mysterious plague. The streets were empty that evening, save for one man wearing a tattered coat, who was looping through blocks of boarded and burned-out buildings on a three-speed bicycle.

I stopped into a Hispanic bakery to pick up some sweets for Marta and her daughter. The overly friendly proprietor packed me a box of frosted donuts while I looked out the plate-glass window to a landscape that seemed both barren and strangely alive.

The door to Marta's building was metal and glass with the number stamped in black. There was no small decoration or frill to offer welcome. The dark, narrow staircase was littered with empty bottles and cans and smelled, predictably, of urine. On the third floor, Marta waited, holding her door open with her hip. Her hair was freshly washed and styled into a flip, and she'd changed clothes since I'd seen her at the center. Her apartment smelled of Pine Sol and Febreze. Her daughter ran up to me, her tightly woven braids slapping at her shoulders.

"This is my teacher," Marta told her, as she led me into the immaculate apartment. "I did all of this in one weekend," she told me, sweeping her arm to indicate the decor. Just days after she was robbed, she explained, she got a $1,200 income tax refund check from the IRS in the mail. The refund was the result of a four-month stint doing filing and typing in a Job Corps program. She used the money to refurnish her apartment, she said, pointing out the green velvet floor-length curtains she'd purchased for $7.99 in a thrift shop and the floor lamp in the corner she'd repainted so it looked like new. With the rest of the money she'd bought the matching sofa and chair, the television, a glass-topped table, and a mirror in a carved frame—in short, everything in the room. We sat on the sofa across from the brand-new television set that was left on but ignored, and Marta began her story. I already knew the broad outline from her writing in our autobiography class, but I listened as she filled in the details.

She was born in Hartford, Connecticut in 1982, the last of four children born to parents who were addicted to heroin. By the time she was five, the Department of Social Services placed her and her siblings with relatives. She and one of her brothers moved in with their grandmother. Those were maybe the most stable years of her life. She went to school and she helped take care of her grandmother, who had diabetes. She never saw either of her parents. Her father was in and out of jail, and her mother was eventually placed in a nursing home because the effects of long-term drug use left her body wasted.

When she was fifteen, Marta got into a fight with another girl, and as an act of revenge, began flirting with the girl's boyfriend. Flirting escalated to "hooking up," and Marta soon became pregnant. Without discussing her decision with anyone, she dropped out of ninth grade. "Everyone else was going to parties and going to the mall," she said. "And I've been struggling ever since."

Eight months after her daughter was born, her grandmother died of diabetes, and Marta was on her own. She lived first in a homeless shelter, then moved in with her grandmother's longtime companion, the man whom she has come to call *abuelo*, Spanish for "grandfather." She decided to try to mend her relationship with her baby's father, who had been seeing other young women. Her boyfriend said he was moving to Florida, and despite her grandfather's warnings not to go, she followed him.

"I was young and naive," Marta said of her efforts to make things work with a young man who seemed bent on cheating. "I wanted to be a family. Everyone wants that, right?"

In Florida, she quickly found that the change of scenery didn't change her boyfriend. He continued to cheat on her, and Marta finally decided to leave him. She tried to find work, but employers required a state ID, which she didn't have. Nor did she have the money to send for an original copy of her birth certificate, with which she might be able to get one. Broke and depressed, she found herself on the streets of Dania, a city outside of Fort Lauderdale, when a stranger approached her.

"He saw me crying one day, and he was like, 'Why are you crying?' At first I said, 'Don't talk to me,'" but he kept insisting he could help. "How can you help me, are you God or something?'" she finally asked him.

As it turned out, he was a drug dealer. He offered her four hundred dollars a week to work for him bagging cocaine. Marta accepted the offer, and used her pay to rent an apartment for herself and her daughter, soon saving enough to fly home. "That wasn't the life I chose for me," she said.

Back in Holyoke, Marta was broke again. But this time she was determined not to depend on drug money for a living. She moved back into a shelter and supported herself and her daughter with checks from welfare. It was at the welfare office that she first heard about The Care Center.

She took the GED again and again, but couldn't pass the math section. Finally, the center provided her with a volunteer tutor, who bought Marta a math book that she could take home and study. Nearly a year later, she took the test again. It was while she was waiting for the results that her apartment was robbed.

Just a few days later, she pulled a large yellow envelope out of her mailbox. "What bad news is this?" she thought, before pulling it open. When she saw what was inside, she began to cry again. Inside were her test results: she had passed. "I was screaming and crying right there in the hallway. Man, was I happy."

By the time Marta finished her story, her daughter had drifted off to sleep on the couch beside her. "I'd better start dinner," Marta said. She pulled cans and boxes out of cabinets and checked on a pot of chicken thighs simmering on the stove. She swiftly opened cans and stirred spices into the steaming pots. Soon the kitchen was filled with the smells of rice and beans and garlic and onions. Marta propped the door open, leaned out into the hallway, and lit a cigarette. For a moment, stillness and quiet descended on the small rooms. Now with Marta's voice no longer crowding out the despair of her surroundings, I could sense how fragile her hope really was.

"It's so hard, Tzivia," she said. "Sometimes I think about just giving up. Packing my things and just going far away."

—

I was eager to return to my carrel at the library, where I would thread another reel of microfilm and fill the lighted screen with square after square of the heavy black ink and yellowed background of crumbling newspaper pages. Under the spell of the whirring film, I would return to the year 1928, when Elizabeth Towne was campaigning to be the first female mayor of Holyoke.

For nearly a month now, each time I visited the library I'd request a new roll of film, load it into the viewer, and lose myself for an hour at a time in the colorful history of Towne's political career.

I began my reading with the 1926 edition of the newspaper, the year Towne first ran for a seat on the city's Board of Aldermen, and planned to continue reading right through 1928, when she lost her final political race in Holyoke. But even though I knew the ending of the story, I was drawn into its unfolding and caught up in its suspense as if the conclusion had yet to be written.

On this day, I knew my reading would take me to the election and the finale of Towne's mayoral race. So it took a great deal of self-restraint to drive past the library and go first to the bank. I needed cash to finish my research; it cost a quarter a page to print from the microfilm viewer, and I didn't even have a dollar in my wallet.

As soon as I pushed through the glass door and into the bank, I was sorry I hadn't brought along my ATM card. The snaking line folded back on itself three times. There must have been twenty people waiting for three tellers. In addition, children and grandparents sat restlessly on the cushioned benches under the windows while they waited for family members who were inching their way forward in line.

"First Monday of the month," I heard a teller explain apologetically to a white man in a business suit, whose body posture, even from behind, broadcast his impatience. His shoulders tight, neck stiff, he pocketed his receipt and made his way to the door. With him gone, I noticed I was the only white person in line. I was about to give up—I could probably find enough quarters in my car, at the bottom of my glove box or under my seat, to pay for at least a few printouts. But just as I was deciding to leave, I heard someone say *hola*, in a high-pitched, familiar voice.

I looked up to see Maria, the custodian from The Care Center. She was farther up in line, one or two people away from the teller.

"Hello," I answered. Now, having been recognized, I felt trapped. If I left now, Maria would think I was like the white man who had drawn bitter stares from the people on line. "He thinks he's too good for us," they were probably thinking. Since Maria spoke no English, and I no Spanish, I couldn't even finesse a sudden exit with a hasty excuse: Look at the time! I have a dentist's appointment across town in five minutes! I'm late, I'd better run—

Maria took her turn at the window. I saw her slip a blue envelope with a plastic window through to the teller, who pulled out a yellow check bearing a government insignia. Was she old enough to receive Social Security payments? She didn't seem to have a disability, and she wouldn't be receiving Aid to Families with Dependent Children, I thought. Or was she? I looked around at the other people on line. Everyone was holding a similar blue envelope with a yellow check inside. At the counter now, a woman was collecting twenty-dollar bills that the teller was dealing out as if this were a game of cards. The checks must arrive on the first of the month. That's why the line was so long today, I thought. I watched as young women my students' age, middle-aged women wearing cheap raincoats that could be no protection against the bitter cold outside, and women who might be grandmothers in puffy black boots and thick knit caps one by one handed over their checks and pocketed a handful of bills. Only women, I noticed, as the line moved slowly ahead.

Maria collected her money and turned to wave to me before heading for the door.

I was surprised to feel resentful of this line of women carrying their envelopes to the tellers' windows. I was surprised to notice myself thinking, "Why can't they work?" All of this even after my recent conversation with Marta, during which I cursed welfare for threatening to cut short her benefits. Even with all I knew of poverty and racism—even thinking of my students who'd gotten their GEDs and now had spent months going from interview to interview for jobs as customer service reps at discount stores and door-to-door kitchen knife saleswomen and data entry clerks for seven dollars an hour (if they were lucky)—and then not getting those dead-end jobs—even knowing all of that, I looked out on the line ahead of me and worried that my shoulders were growing as tense as those of the white man who had walked away, his camel-hair coat belted tightly around his waist.

Finally, it was my turn. I withdrew fifty dollars and left the bank. I decided, despite the frigid day, to leave my car parked downtown and walk the few blocks to the library. I hoped I'd be able to walk off my small-mindedness in the process.

If I could so easily work up ill feelings toward women like the ones I just left in the bank, if I could feel hostile toward them for receiving welfare and disability payments in order to keep their families fed and in decent clothes, then what about the vast majority of people across the country who called them freeloaders and lazy breeders—or who simply voted against candidates who wanted to increase the minimum wage or fought to defend welfare and social service budgets?

I remembered Maria cleaning around me in my office a few months earlier, and how she had muttered, "*No entiende nada. No entiende nada.*" She doesn't understand anything. She doesn't understand anything.

At the library, Devon greeted me. "Ready for the next reel?" he asked, as he led me to the tall metal cabinet whose drawers held hundreds of small cardboard boxes, each of which contained another month's worth of old newspapers recorded on strips of film and wound around a plastic spool.

"Getting a lot of good stuff?" he asked as he pulled open the drawer labeled 1928 and moved aside so I could find the spool marked "November."

I put my tote bag and pocketbook on an empty chair next to what had become my regular machine and expertly threaded the film under, over, and through the maze of plastic rollers the way Devon had taught me. I flicked on the power button and listened to the sound of the film snapping into place and whirring onto the take-up reel. I fast-forwarded to the spot where I had left off the last time I'd sat here: November 11, 1928.

It was three days before the election and once again Elizabeth Towne stepped up to the podium to advance her mayoral campaign. Just two years before, Towne, a woman and an outsider, had glided into a seat on the Board of Alderman as if taking her place at a banquet—the first woman in the city's history to do so. But her bid for mayor was not going as smoothly.

This rally, her last public event before the vote, was her chance to make her positions clear, and put her campaign back on track. She stood at the dais of the high school auditorium, inhaling the air, which was heavy with the scent of cigarette smoke and damp wool. A quick tally of filled rows multiplied by the number of seats in each told her that a hundred or more people had turned out. Not bad, considering that the newspapers were saying Holyoke had tired of this campaign before it began. The city's voters had just been through a national election (putting Herbert Hoover into office), and lacked the attention for a local race—or so the editorials moaned. But Towne, who was herself smarting from the spectacular defeat of Alfred Smith, the Democrat on whose campaign she'd worked feverishly for months, could see many of her supporters filling the seats before her. Among them was, of course, Chester Struble, her forty-five-year-old son who was the managing editor of the *Nautilus*, as well as her campaign chairman. It was he who had advertised tonight's rally as "something else entirely new in the line of political rallies."

The icy rain falling outside hadn't kept the crowd away. After all, for the first time in Holyoke's history, a woman was on the ballot for mayor. And if that weren't enough, the other two candidates were the city's current mayor and a former mayor. The sitting mayor was Fred G. Burnham, whose name Towne couldn't pronounce without a curl of disdain winding around the syllables. Nor could she reconcile the injustice of the man's apparent popularity with the voters, despite having achieved nothing beyond paving mile after mile of roadway. Meanwhile, the city's children were learning in a school that was nothing but a catastrophe waiting to happen, with hastily built classrooms and stairwells that might just as well be wicks to carry fire from top to bottom, should an open flame happen to catch.

The other candidate, John F. Cronin, was the previous mayor of Holyoke. He'd done a good enough job, so why not just take a seat on the sidelines now and let some new blood have at it? Towne wondered. But no answers would be forthcoming on this evening, as neither of Towne's rivals bothered to attend the rally. Instead, Towne shared the stage with various candidates for open seats on the Board of Aldermen.

At sixty-three, Towne stood tall and inhaled deeply before she addressed her audience: "I want to extend to the voters of Holyoke an invitation to join with me in creating an administration of real public service. By this, I mean an administration dedicated not to any particular group or race, not to the reward and advancement of political friends or favorites, not to the interest alone of the business men, but which would be dedicated to the home and children and worker as well, which would in short serve all the people of Holyoke without fear or prejudice or special favor."[32]

Towne was reading from a prepared speech, but as the night progressed she veered with increasing frequency from the words printed on the ream of paper before her. She inserted asides, explanations, digs, and comments. But as she spoke, the crowd grew restless. She heard mutterings, words she couldn't quite make out, coming from one corner of the room.

She continued with her speech. "My first point of departure from the administration was the mayor's attitude toward the Gas and Electric Plant," she said.

"Why don't you tell the people why you're really running?" Before she searched out the speaker in the crowd, she knew the voice. She had heard Martin Spies raise his objections to her political aspirations often in the two years since winning her seat on the Board of Aldermen. The first female alderman-at-large, she silently gloated. And now, here she stood: the first female candidate for mayor. And she could be the first female mayor, too. She could see it in her mind's eye; she could see herself seated at the majestic desk in Room One of City Hall. How often had she visualized this as she looked out her second-floor window, past the flowering trees on her lawn and southward, across the sandlots and rooftops to the clock tower that rose in the distance, above City Hall? If she could envision it, she could achieve it, she told herself.

But Spies wasn't going to make it easy. Three weeks before, at her first campaign rally of this election, he'd been present, and the heckling had begun.

"Admit what's really got a bee in your bonnet," Spies said. "It isn't the mayor's position on Gas and Electric and it isn't even the new junior high School." Spies turned away from Towne and directed his comments at the crowd. Sweeping his hand in an arc as he spoke, he said, "It's a ploy for publicity, and that's all it is."

"Mr. Spies, you do not have the floor," Towne reprimanded. "And in any case, as the publisher of an internationally known magazine, I have all the publicity I could ask for."

"And that's publicity Holyoke doesn't need. A mayor who is the high priestess of New Thought! Holyoke would be a laughing stock. Why don't you go home and tell your readers to vote telepathically without even going to the polls," he chided.

The sounds of choked guffaws gave way to full belly laughs.

"Mr. Spies, I ask you to take your seat," Towne's son, Chester, admonished.

"Mr. Struble, by all means. But first, let me ask what your stake in your mother's aspirations might be. Mightn't you be in line for a powerful position if she were to be elected?"

"And then who would run my business?" Towne bellowed.

"Why don't you go back and run your business then, and leave Holyoke's business to *real* Holyokers?" Spies barked back.

"Why don't you sit down, fathead!" The voice came from somewhere in the rear of the hall. Towne tried to see who it was but couldn't. The audience roared with laughter and hooted their agreement. Spies tugged at his jacket and made for the door.

Elizabeth Towne began her political career in Holyoke in 1926, when Calvin Coolidge was president, and some two dozen women were on the ballot for seats in Congress nationwide. That year, in addition to her regular duties as editor of *Nautilus*, a wife, mother of two, and grandmother of four, Towne had assumed the editorship of the International New Thought Alliance's *New Thought Bulletin*. As if that weren't enough, she was also finishing her two-year term as international lecturer for the same organization, and with her husband, Wil-

liam, attended a New Thought conference in London, all while remaining active in local organizations, including the Holyoke League
of Women's Voters. Now, she could add to her list of titles and duties:
alderman. She was the pioneering woman in Holyoke politics, and the
first married woman alderman in the state (other women had already
become aldermen in Woburn and Springfield).

The year she took office, 1927, seemed to be a year for women
attempting "unwomanly" things. A female doctor swam the English
Channel; Ruth Elder took off in a monoplane from Roosevelt Field on
Long Island in a doomed cross-Atlantic journey; and England elected
its first female mayor. Closer to home, Helena Hill Weed, a grandmother, ran for mayor in Norwalk, Connecticut (but was defeated). In
Concord, New Hampshire, Miss Helen Gwendolyn Jones, twenty-
four, ran for mayor, and the newspapers assured that the campaign did
not "interfere with household duties."[33]

Holyoke welcomed Towne to the board with a mix of friendly
acceptance and skepticism. "Were the women hypnotized? Looks like
it," a post-election roundup in the local newspaper quipped. And in
the same column: "The Board of Alderman of 1927 is in for a good
many midnight sessions with Alderman Towne still talking."

Towne herself was walking on air. She gave the news to her extended family of *Nautilus* readers in the February issue of her magazine: "Congratulations are in order! On December 7th I was elected
Alderman-at-Large in the city of Holyoke…And I came out at the
top of the list of seven Aldermen-at-Large…The women say that they
are the ones who put me in! And the men are saying that it was they
who did it! But just between you and me, I rather think that they both
had a finger in the pie."

As a politician, Towne treated the city newspaper as if it were one
of her own periodicals. She became a frequent contributor to the
"Safety Valve" column, an informal letters-to-the-editor-type forum,
opining on everything from automobile safety to new laws creating
jury service for women. Her (sometimes daily) letters to the editor
ran to more than a thousand words in some cases. Unhappy with the
bidding process for cement and coal in the city, she wrote an open
letter to the Board of Public Works, enumerating her concerns and
demanding point-by-point responses, which were also published in
excruciating detail.

Six months into her tenure as alderman, Towne gushed in the *Nautilus* that politics offered one more opportunity to express New Thought principles through service. "So far the biggest devil I have found in politics lies outside the political machinery, among those who go about telling each other how dirty politics is and how they would not touch politics at any price!" She said that she found among the twenty-one aldermen on the board "everybody human, as well as divine."[34]

From the moment she took office as alderman, Towne's run for mayor seemed inevitable. "Mrs. Elizabeth Towne is not only the pioneer woman alderman but she is quite likely to be the pioneer woman mayor," a columnist wrote in the first days following her election.

In taking the challenge two years later, Towne had her work cut out for her. Nationwide, the first female mayor was elected in 1887, when Susana Madora Salter, age twenty-seven, was placed on the ballot in Argonia, Kansas—as a joke.[35] The gag was meant to embarrass women who were "stepping out of line" and demanding their rights, but the joke backfired when Salter won. In 1926, the year Towne became alderman, Bertha Landes became the first female mayor of Seattle, and the first female mayor of a major U.S. city.[36]

Towne would need to rally all of her powers of positive thinking—and all her financial resources—to win her mayoral race. In Holyoke the population had begun its decline, and one of the city's largest mills had closed. Towne estimated that her campaign would cost $5,200, the equivalent of the mayor's annual salary. This was a record-breaking figure in Holyoke's politics, and Towne would pay for it out of her own funds; she refused to accept money that might make her beholden to special interests.

Save for Towne's presence, the race was considered among the quietest in the city's history. As if trying to make up for her opponents' lack of enthusiasm, Towne campaigned at full throttle. She took out quarter- and half-page ads on a regular basis, and published lengthy letters to the Safety Valve. She held several political rallies and when the newspaper didn't cover them to her satisfaction, she wrote her own articles, referring to herself in the third person and including quotes and observations. Reports of her speeches at political rallies often noted that Alderman Towne addressed issues "at great length."

By contrast, her archrival, Mayor Burnham, couldn't be bothered to show up at political rallies hosted by his opponents. He issued one political statement during his campaign and attended a single rally, just days before the election. When Burnham finally did speak up, he used the opportunity to slam Towne. Two days before the voters would take to the polls, he finally addressed the accusations and criticisms Towne had been lobbing his way for weeks:

"The vagaries, hallucinations and arguments of the 'New Thought' mind temporarily diverted from their proper channels into problems political, are alike inexplanable [sic] and like the ways of Divine Providence, passeth all understanding,"[37] he said.

Towne rebutted in another letter to the Safety Valve: "Though I may look up, as well as down; though I may look forward with enthusiasm, my two feet are planted firmly upon the earth and I am very much on the job,"[38] she wrote.

Although no one seemed to think Towne would win, her campaign was still considered formidable—that is, until the votes were counted.

After showing little interest in the campaign during the weeks before the election, Holyoke's voters turned out in record numbers. Of the nearly 20,000 who came to the polls, more than half voted for Burnham. A healthy 7,490 voted for former Mayor Cronin. Only 478 cast a vote for Towne.

In the aftermath of his landslide victory, an elated Burnham greeted hundreds of well-wishers who turned out at his office early the next morning with messages of congratulations. Letters and messages poured in even more quickly, including a letter of support from Holyoke's famous Siamese twins, Margaret and Mary Gibbs.

Towne meanwhile issued the tersest message of her political career—perhaps of her entire literary career. Her eighty-eight word statement read:

> I congratulate Mr. Burnham on being elected by the majority of votes and I wish him every success.
>
> Naturally I am sorry I did not win yesterday's election, but I was not greatly surprised.
>
> 'They said' no mayor could be elected without 'the machine' but I had hoped it could be done.

Two Holyoke men politicians have tried it, one received 67 votes, if I remember it, and the other a hundred and something. The woman did not do so badly by comparison. I shall not try again.[39]

———

Having completely lost myself in the story of Towne's political defeat, I now found myself slumped into the wooden chair in front of the microfilm reader feeling devastated. I had known, of course, that Towne didn't win the mayor's race, but I hadn't known how badly she had lost it. But more than that, her final statement, "I shall not try again," echoed in my mind. The high priestess of positive thinking had given up.

I rewound the film, slipped the spool into its cardboard box, and left it on Devon's desk. Despondent, I made my way out of the library and trudged downtown to my car.

I turned onto the street where I had parked, only to find that the space where my car had been parked was empty. As I looked at the vacant rectangle, outlined by a crust of icy snow, I felt a stunned, dizzy sensation in my gut. I took a minute to make sure I was on the right block, that I knew just where I had parked, that there was no other explanation. There was not. My car was gone.

My fingers were turning numb from the cold. I stepped inside the bank to warm up before walking the next couple of blocks to the police station. By now the teller's line was down to just a couple of customers, but my anger was rising. How dare they? How dare *they*? I felt the horror of what I was thinking, but I rode the heat of my rage as I strode to the police station.

Inside, I burst into tears as I told an indifferent officer that my car had been stolen. He ignored my tears and took my information. Everything about his bored manner told me that this was just a routine matter, that I was naive to have expected anything but this. "Do you have a ride home?" he asked. I shook my head. He offered to call me a cab.

"I'll walk," I said, as if somehow my refusal of his offer to call me a cab would punish him, not me. The digital thermometer on the clock outside the bank read 4°F.

I would walk to The Care Center, I decided. That was much closer than my house, and someone there could give me a ride the rest of the way home. But just a block from the police station I saw my car. It was driving past, slowly. I double-checked to be sure I was right. The license plate confirmed it. That was my car, with a young man with black hair and dark skin wearing a beige-colored down jacket at the wheel.

"That's my car!" I shouted, as I began to chase him. "Stop!" I yelled, as passersby stared but didn't interfere. I ran for three blocks, past the park, through an old cobblestoned alley, and past the pizza place and Chinese food restaurant. My feet were pinched and achy in my leather-soled flats and my lungs burned with each gulp of frozen air I swallowed. But I kept running, and thanks to traffic and a red light that slowed the driver, I was able to keep my car in sight. I heard myself yelling profanities as I ran. "I worked hard to buy that fucking car! Get a job and buy your own!"

Out of breath, with the car slipping around the next corner, I stopped at a parking garage, where the attendant sat in his glassed-in booth. "Call the police!" I said, my lungs in wild pain now from the exertion and the cold. "That's my car, that man stole it!"

The attendant ordered me to sit down while he called the police. In minutes an officer arrived and I pointed to the street my car had just turned down. It didn't take him long to find it (the dashboard ruined, window shattered, ignition broken), and cuff the driver.

You[40]

You went from darkness to light
You went through storms and
hurricanes hearing people saying
you can't make it in this life
for a while believing it was true.
You felt like the whole world
was ending. You seen your
whole life flash before
your eyes. You went through
cold, muddy nights all alone thinking
is someone there for you
instead of you being there
for someone else? You left behind
dolls, dollhouses, Big Wheels.
You moved on to pregnancy, having
cravings for McDonalds, shrimp rolls,
to buying baby clothes to having
no patience. Not wanting no
more kids, wanting birth control, looking
at life in a whole new and
different way. Knowing that
life is hard and not easy.

Knowing being a mother
was going to be hard.
Knowing the father was not
going to be there.
Knowing I can do this.

Knowing it is going to get hard
before it gets better.
Knowing one day you will
be and become the person
you want to be.

CHAPTER EIGHT

I'M GOING TO FIGHT YOU

ANA SAT SLOUCHED IN A FOLDING CHAIR IN THE OFFICE, her arms crossed over her chest. She wore a pursed-lip smile on her face, which I took as a challenge to ask what was new.

"Didn't you hear? One of our students killed herself last night," she said.

I searched Ana's face. Was she joking? No, she wouldn't dare. "Who?" I asked, but Ana refused to tell me and I didn't want to start guessing; that seemed morbid, but I needed to know who had died. I was getting more and more upset. Finally, Ana told me: "It was Julissa."

Julissa had a face and body Hollywood would pay a king's ransom for, if only they could have found her there in downtown Holyoke. She had copper-colored highlights in her cascading hair and she spoke in puffs of smoke, like a Spanish Marilyn Monroe. She hadn't been in class for months—and now this.

Ana told me this news, then went back to what she was doing, as if she'd just told me that snow had been forecast for that afternoon, or that one of the vans was late picking up students. My face contorted into tears. Then I was furious. "How can you be so nonchalant about this?" I sputtered.

"Calm down, Tzivia. You're making a big deal out of nothing," she replied, in her deep, confident voice.

I forced myself to follow Ana's lead and make my face impassive.

It had been one of those ordinary and shocking dreams: realistic in its setting, outrageous in its details, and I had forgotten it as soon as I opened my eyes. I may never have remembered it all, except that Ana, unknowingly, brought it up.

We were sitting in the lunchroom at one of the round tables that a group of girls had just vacated, finishing off barely warm slices of pizza and discussing plans for a student recognition ceremony. During the ceremony, Ana was explaining, the teachers would distribute pins honoring the girls' achievements. The ceremony was meant to give each young woman a sense of accomplishment. After all, even if we were lucky, only about a fifth would actually graduate that June. The GED certificate, we wanted this ceremony to demonstrate, isn't the only benchmark of success.

Ana and I soon found ourselves disagreeing over how to handle the distribution of the pins. Would each student receive just one award for a special achievement, such as excellence in sports, writing, or art? Or should the girls receive as many pins as they deserved?

"The pins only cost sixty cents apiece; why not give the girls as many as they've earned?" Ana argued.

"But that would dilute the impact. They won't mean anything anymore," I countered.

We went back and forth on this, each digging deeper into her position. I knew that even while we were arguing with the full passion of our beliefs over this relatively small detail, we weren't so much fighting as jousting. Ana and I both liked to win. On the other hand, I knew Ana was my supervisor and that on some level she was serious about wanting me to give in to her point of view. As if to prove this, she finally warned, "I'll use my *bruja* powers and send you bad dreams if you don't back off." She delivered the threat with her arms crossed over her chest and that pursed-lip smile.

"But you *did* send me a dream last night," I said, only then beginning to recall the nightmare I'd had about Julissa.

"Did I?" Ana was clearly impressed with herself. "In advance! I must have known you'd cross me today. Boy, I'm good."

At first I could only recall glimpses, but as I began to describe the dream to her the details flooded back. It was only as I was relating it that I realized what it had been about: I'd dreamt of Julissa's violent death and Ana's blasé response because my students' lives upset me, but to do my work I had to act as if it was all okay: Marta's apartment being robbed, the theft of my own car, Solmary's building burning down.

Just a few days before one girl had told me that she'd come home Friday night to find a crack addict standing in her kitchen. He'd broken into her apartment and was grabbing the frozen pork chops from her freezer. She laughed hysterically as she described the way he held a knife to her throat as he made his way out the door with the stolen meat. Her appreciation for the absurdity of the crime and the banality of being terrified by the blade of desperation were braided into her impossible laughter. And when I assigned a poem about walking outside at night, the girls just shook their heads. "We don't want to go out on the street at night, Miss. We're not crazy," Crystelle said. Sylvie explained that she liked winter better than summer because in the warm weather she and her sisters never left their apartment for fear of the dealers congregating on the corners. At least in winter no one felt like going out, anyway. Students described plastic bags of heroin dropped in playgrounds, triple-locked doors, and shattered windows they couldn't afford to replace. Police raids, foster homes, younger brothers tying on do-rags and heading out to the streets. Lovers who had stabbed people; brothers who sold and bought drugs; the threat of having their welfare cases closed; the hopelessness of no money for milk, let alone a book; and the plotting involved in buying a single pair of shoes some days, while a good street-corner deal on another day would net a wide-screen color TV. Even the scent of cheap votive candles, burning in their apartments to cover up the smell of cigarettes or weed, seemed sinister to me then.

I told Ana that I thought it better not to know too much about their lives. How could I make them learn the definition of words like *metaphor, stanza* and *cliché* if I let myself think about everything they were trying to forget? As I put into words thoughts, which up until that moment I'd barely sorted out for myself, I felt my cheeks burning and tears threatened to burst from my eyes. "I guess the problem is that as I get to know them, I know their stories too, and that includes all this pain and sadness and unfairness," I said.

I remembered being a teenager myself, and how the more I saw of the injustice in the world the more furious I became. And for me, a middle-class white girl growing up in the suburbs of Long Island, most of those injustices were being perpetrated against others, not myself. How much anger must my students be carrying...or working hard to suppress? I wondered.

"I have to do the same thing," Ana said. "How could I discipline a student for something as trivial as making a cell phone call during class if I were to let myself think about everything she's got to face when she walks out these doors?" She looked straight at me while she spoke, and I wondered if she could see the emotions churning behind my mask of calm. Could she sense that I was a breath away from breaking down there in the lunchroom, amid the empty pizza boxes piled on tables and the half-finished plastic bottles of Sunny-D and Pepsi? I wondered if she would say now, as she had just a few months ago, that I was hiding behind a fortress, and that she couldn't see what was inside me beyond those walls. Or was there perhaps a fissure now, through which she could peek?

But there was no time to find out. Carmen, the school's secretary, strode into the room to tell Ana that there was a phone call for her in the office. I took the opportunity to gather up my tote bag and make my way upstairs to our staff meeting.

———

It was now March. If we were to publish a literary magazine before graduation we'd have to get serious, I told the students in my afternoon class. Despite some talk about the idea of making a magazine, we hadn't accomplished much yet. Sonia, who was wearing a metallic-blue ski jacket, stuffed her hands into her pockets and eyed me skeptically.

"I know it's hard to believe it will take so long," I said, "but trust me, we have a lot of work to do, and we're only meeting once a week."

The first task, as I saw it, was to form this reluctant band of students into an editorial board with a focused intent. Our group included Esme, who had the literary grace of a gangster spraying the page with bullets of profanity; Crystelle, who was only in the workshop because there'd been no room in the computer class; Luz, who still flinched anytime anyone spoke directly to her; Jazmin, with raven black hair and a sullen expression; Suleika, who would gladly have taken over as teacher, and who seemed to think she'd do a far better job at it; Sonia, who could barely keep her eyes open, having been up until daybreak on any given night with one or more of her three children; and Carmen who, despite her meticulously ordered appearance, with powder blue sneakers that matched her powder blue nails and fuzzy sweater, could hardly put a sentence together on the page. Rhonda had agreed to join our group as my associate editor, and I was grateful to see her sitting at one of the desks I'd arranged in a circle to give the meeting a more democratic feel.

I handed out copies of our production schedule, which included sessions for writing, selecting poetry and artwork, typing the poems into the computer, creating a cover design, choosing typefaces, editing and submitting the manuscript to the printer, and planning a reading and celebration. Then I told the group we'd spend this meeting getting to know each other better.

I gave each student an index card and asked them to write one line stating a quality they possessed or a part of their personality that they were bringing to the group, which would help us see how strong we were together. They didn't need to put their name on the card, I said. When they were done, I'd collect the statements and we'd put them together into one poem, which would tell us who we were as a board.

Relieved that they only had to write one sentence, the girls eagerly picked up pens and pencils. While the last ones were finishing up, I began to read the completed cards silently, to myself. "I am the best mother I can be." "I'm a real friend, not a back stabber." "I am strong like a mother lion." "I am all of the colors of the rainbow." I recognized Luz's spidery script on the next card. She had written: "I am gay and proud of it." I felt my face flush as I shifted to the next card.

I pretended to be absorbed in what I was reading, but all I could do was wonder about what Luz had written. Had she found out I was gay and written this to get a reaction from me? Was this quiet student just looking for attention? Had she written it on a dare, provoked perhaps by her new friend Jazmin? Or could this be as it appeared, a proclamation made by the young woman trapped behind that suffocating silence? No, I decided as I mechanically collected the last of the students' cards, it couldn't be true. Luz had an infant daughter and a boyfriend to whom she had written endless, pained love poems. Or at least I'd assumed those poems had been to a *boy*friend. I tried to pull up lines from my memory. "I didn't know I loved your lips / until they finally kissed me,"[41] and "Red, how I want you back. / Red roses, dying slowly and slowly. / Your silky skin and your sweet soft lips…"[42] There had been no pronouns in those poems, I now realized. Writing and speaking about one's life without the use of pronouns is a skill every gay man and woman quickly masters. How could I have missed it? But then I was sure I remembered overhearing Luz complain to Jazmin about her baby's father, and saying how she wished he'd come back.

"Let's hear them," Rhonda prompted. I looked up, wishing I could have a telepathic conference with her to ask her what I should do. I could just skip over Luz's card and pretend I didn't see it, I thought.

I snuck a glance at Luz. She and Jazmin were whispering and giggling. Even if she'd written it as a joke, I should read it aloud to show her I didn't think it was anything to be embarrassed about. I would treat her statement as I would any other. Like Rhonda's for example, which said, "I am half Irish and half Puerto Rican." Or Sonia's, which said, "I am wise." If Luz was trying to force me out of my silence on the subject, I'd take the challenge. It would be a relief, I thought, to finally get the issue out in the open and face the consequences.

"Let's go, Teacher," Suleika prodded, "everyone's finished."

"Okay," I said, tapping the cards on the desk to make a neat stack. "We're just about ready." Maybe Luz really was gay, I considered, as I pretended to correct the punctuation on the card in front of me. And if she was gay, the worst thing I could possibly do was silence her by not reading her statement along with the others.

"Here we go," I said.

"Finally," Suleika sighed.

As I read each statement I focused on keeping my voice steady and neutral. When I got to Luz's I read each word slowly. "I am gay, and proud of it."

I tried to move ahead to the next card but Esme shouted, "Who the fuck wrote that?"

"It doesn't matter," I answered. "These are lines we might use in a group poem. The point is to learn who we are as an editorial board. Individual authorship isn't important right now." I tried again to read the next card.

"That's disgusting," Sonia muttered.

I was about to launch into a lecture on gay pride, when Suleika intervened. "My uncle from Springfield is gay. He's the best uncle I have. There's nothing wrong with it."

"That's right, it's no one's damn business," Esme said, with an authoritative nod of her head. "But," she added, "I still want to know who wrote it."

"Whoever wrote it should know we don't mind," Suleika said.

Rhonda looked at me and smiled as if to say, "They're cooler than we thought."

"I know who wrote it," Crystelle said. "It's the teacher."

I felt my pores open as sweat cascaded in rivers beneath my shirt.

"Damn! You're right. It's Rhonda!" Esme exclaimed. Crystelle smiled, knowingly.

Rhonda burst out laughing. "After some of the dates I've had with men lately, I wish it was me," she said. "But, it's not. And like Tzivia said, it's not even important who wrote it. Let's keep going so we can hear everyone's statements."

"The point," I said, regaining my ability to behave like a teacher, "is to take pride in all aspects of who we are. We can certainly be proud of whoever had the courage to share this with us." I finished reading the rest of the statements and when it was finally time for the students to leave, I stopped Luz as she gathered her things. Jazmin paused briefly at the door, then disappeared. Rhonda sat at the desk in the far corner, trying to look busy, but clearly determined to see this drama unfold.

"Look," I said to Luz, "if what you wrote on your card was meant to be a joke, I want you to know these things are serious to me." I looked over at Rhonda, who was pretending not to listen. I wanted to catch her eye so I could signal her to come over and bail me out, but she feigned concentrated interest in the papers she was reading. I looked back at Luz, whose expression I still could not read. "On the other hand, if you are serious and you really are gay, I want you to know you can talk to me or to any of the staff here if you need support."

"It wasn't a joke," Luz said flatly.

"Then I'm proud of you for having the courage to share that information with me and with the class."

Jazmin leaned into the room and Rhonda stood and began to collect stray index cards and pencils students had left behind.

"I'll look forward to seeing you next week," I told Luz. "I'm glad you're on our editorial board." She nodded, and walked over to where Jazmin was waiting.

As soon as they disappeared into the hallway Rhonda erupted into conversation. "Wasn't that great! Weren't you impressed with how the other students reacted? Can you believe it? Luz of all people! I'd never have guessed!"

"Yeah," I said, dropping into the chair Luz had just vacated. "But what about the fact that they pegged you as the lesbian and not me? What was that about?"

"Maybe it's a sign that I should switch teams," Rhonda said, and raised her hand for a high five. I gave her hand a perfunctory slap and shook my head. For me it was one more piece of evidence that the students couldn't perceive in me any of the subtle differences that define a person's uniqueness. To them I was just white. Just other.

"What about Luz, though?" Rhonda was saying. "Maybe you should check in with her counselor to see how it's going for her. Being gay in the Puerto Rican community can be pretty rough."

Rhonda was right. Why was I thinking about myself when I should be thinking of Luz?

"And you know," Rhonda said, "it might help her to have a role model. Someone she can look up to; someone who is gay, and who has a good, happy life." Rhonda widened her eyes and used them to punctuate her sentence. She wanted to be sure that what might have sounded like an off-handed suggestion was, in fact, a direct order.

Luz wasn't in class the next day, and by the time I saw her on Friday afternoon, I'd almost forgotten about my promise to talk to her. But then, as I was standing at the copy machine making copies for the next week's lessons, I saw her come down the stairs. Just before she could turn left and head for the door, I called her name.

"Luz, how's it going?" I asked.

"Fine," she said without smiling.

"I mean, after our workshop Monday. Are you feeling okay about how that went?"

"It was fine," she said, sneaking a glance behind her to see if anyone was close enough to hear our conversation.

"You know, we have something in common," I said.

Finally, Luz looked directly at me. "We do?" she asked.

"Yeah, I could have written the same thing you did."

" *You?*" Luz asked. Her eyebrows lifted with the question and I saw a glint of curiosity in her eyes that I had never noticed before.

"Yes, my girlfriend and I have been together for twelve years. We're raising my daughter together."

" *You?*" Luz repeated, narrowing her eyes. I imagined it was her turn, now, to assess whether *I* was putting *her* on.

"Yeah, me. So I know how hard this might be for you right now."

"It sucks," Luz said.

"If you ever need to talk, just let me know." She nodded, but didn't say anything. "Do you have someone in your life right now?"

"Yeah, the one I wrote all those poems about."

Except for Jazmin and a few other girls who were still lingering in the lunchroom down the hall, the first floor was nearly empty.

"Those were some really powerful poems," I said.

"Thanks," Luz muttered.

The last van must have arrived because the remaining students left the lunchroom and headed out the front door. I watched as Jazmin started in our direction. Luz turned her head to follow my gaze. I wondered if they were seeing each other.

"C'mon Luz, we'll miss the van," Jazmin said.

"The one I wrote the poems for lives in my building. She doesn't go to this school," Luz told me as if in answer to my silent question. Then she joined Jazmin and walked away. Just before they turned the corner Luz whispered something and Jazmin looked over her shoulder in my direction. My secret was out.

At our next editorial board meeting, Luz was wearing a snug-fitting pink terry-cloth running suit with clean white sneakers. Her hair was carefully curled, and her pained grimace was replaced with a smile. She didn't wince when I asked her how she was doing. Instead, she looked me in the eye and said she was doing fine. This time it sounded as though she meant it.

"I guess that's what they mean by coming out," Rhonda observed later. "It's like she's come out of that dark cloud she's been hiding behind and now she's sparkling."

We were meeting in the computer lab, a small room ringed by monitors and keyboards. We were finally ready to begin producing the magazine. Luz had volunteered to design the invitation for our poetry reading, and Esme offered to design a cover. The rest of the editors would start by typing the students' biographical statements, which they'd submitted with their poems. We'd select the poems next week, after I'd made sure everyone who wanted to had submitted something. But first, I wanted to tell the students a little bit about Mrs. Towne and the history of the house.

I started by explaining that Towne had dropped out of school at age fourteen. Sonia looked up, interested. "Me, too," she said. I nodded, and continued to recount the outline of Towne's biography, including her early marriage and divorce. "Back then it was very rare for a married couple to divorce," I said, "and even more unusual for a woman to start her own business and buy her own house." I went on to explain that she was a pioneer in Holyoke's municipal politics and that she'd fought for women's right to vote.

"Women couldn't vote back then?" Suleika asked. "For real?" she continued after I told her it was true.

"People must have thought she was kind of out there," Luz observed.

"That's right," I said. "She was outspoken about what she believed in, and sometimes that got her into trouble."

"If I lived back in the day, I'd be like that, too," Luz said. "I can't just sit around and act like everybody else."

I smiled, and continued with my mini biography. "Another cool thing Mrs. Towne did was to publish a magazine right here in this house," I said.

"A poetry magazine?" Suleika asked.

"Sonia, you saw the magazine at the library, can you tell us anything about it?"

"There were some poems in there, but mostly it was about some weird stuff. It was okay, though. About thinking positive and praying instead of taking medicine."

"Yes," I said. "Mrs. Towne believed in something called New Thought." I explained that New Thought was almost like a religion, and that Mrs. Towne practiced spiritual healing.

"Can we just start making the magazine already?" Crystelle asked.

I looked around at my editors. No one besides Suleika seemed particularly interested in hearing about the history of New Thought. Crystelle was right, I admitted to myself. We were there to make a magazine.

I handed out pages for the students to type, and Rhonda helped Luz get started on the invitation. Esme, meanwhile, was slumped in front of her monitor, having abandoned any pretense of working. On the screen before her was the design she'd begun working on for the cover. She'd scanned into the computer a photograph of a purple house that another student had constructed with cardboard and glue during art class. She combined that with a deco-style border like the ones on some of Towne's old magazines. The juxtaposition of the contemporary image of the house with the antique flourishes brought together the historical and present-day elements of our magazine.

"That's going to be a great cover," I told Esme.

"I can't do any more today," she complained.

"What's the matter?"

Esme tilted her head toward me, frowned, and said, "Ay, I feel sick."

"Is it the pregnancy?" Esme was one month away from delivering her second baby.

"No, I have a cold."

"You know," I told her, "Elizabeth Towne believed you could heal your illnesses just by changing your thoughts and making them more positive," I told her.

"For real?" she asked, without lifting her head. The skepticism in her voice didn't surprise me. After all, every morning a nurse visited the center and students could sign up for an appointment with her. That sign-up sheet was always filled within minutes of being posted in the downstairs lobby. Physical ailments were so prevalent among the students that every time one opened her purse a plastic vial of prescription pills would spill out, along with the inevitable bottles of nail polish, cigarettes, cell phones, and EBT, or welfare, cards. The pills, I learned, were for everything from asthma to anxiety. So, it wasn't surprising when, rather than jump at the idea of trying some spiritual healing to conquer her symptoms, Esme instead asked if she could see the nurse to get some cold medicine.

"She's gone for the day," I said.

Esme sighed.

"Try affirming that you are well," I said. She looked at me blankly. "Tell yourself that your body is healing itself."

Esme sat up and cocked her head at me. She had a way of tucking her chin and tilting her head so as to give me the full benefit of her wide, impatient eyes glaring upward in my direction. "If I try it can I go home early?" she asked.

Towne might have faced similar resistance from one of the young women who spent her days in the typing pool in this house, I thought. Although New Thought had an impressive band of followers nation-wide, it remained outside of the mainstream. In Holyoke, the Townes were said to be the only followers. And a single page from the city's local newspaper from 1910, when *Nautilus* was at its peak in popularity, would have been crowded with ads for medicines, as I knew from my hours in the library studying newspapers from her time. Kerr's Flax-seed Emulsion promised to cure any cough, Dr. Miles's Anti-Pain Pills claimed to be "the only thing that will relieve neuralgia," and an "expert" promised, for a fee, to reveal a "home remedy to cure fat." Page after page was filled with similar advertisements for cures for bronchitis, dandruff, and headaches. By contrast, Towne might have prescribed eating a vegetarian diet, practicing deep breathing exercises, and keeping one's thoughts positive: "The quality of your body, including the brain, determines the quality of your environment. You are your own lord and master, the arbiter of your own destiny," Towne wrote in her 1907 health treatise, "Just How to Wake the Solar Plexus."

New Thought, as it turned out, came of age at around the same time Towne was coming into her own as a woman. At the turn of the twentieth century, and with the coming of mind-boggling inventions like the telegraph, telephone, and electricity, the limitations of the physical world seemed to disappear. At such a time, a philosophy that celebrated the forces of unseen streams of mental energy naturally flourished. New Thought centers were opening around the country, and well-known figures like Frank Baum, creator of *The Wizard of Oz*, R. F. Outcault, Buster Brown's creator, and Elbert Hubbard, who popularized the Arts and Crafts movement, took up the cause.[43]

Towne discovered New Thought as a young mother, when she accompanied her mother-in-law to a lecture by Mrs. George Williams, the wife of Portland's U.S. senator. Mrs. Williams claimed to have been healed by Christian Science, one of the many early off-shoots of the New Thought philosophy, and Towne was so moved by her testimonial that she proceeded to visit Mrs. Williams as often as five times a week for healings and lessons.[44]

An unhappy housewife and mother of two increasingly independent children, Towne became entranced by these new ideas. She was suffering from symptoms of what was then called neurasthenia, a condition marked by nervousness, lack of concentration, worry, and headaches. The malady, which was being diagnosed in large numbers of American women at the time, was said to have been brought about by the demanding pace of "modern civilization." Towne practiced the principles that she was introduced to by Mrs. Williams, and after seeing marked improvement in her own mental state, she began to try to heal others.

However, lacking Towne's powers to banish illness, I gave Esme permission to leave school early that day, and she stayed out sick for the rest of the week. When she returned, she told me she'd tried to cure her cold with positive thinking, but that it was the over-the-counter medication that finally offered her some relief.

At our next meeting, Rhonda was absent, and Crystelle, Suleika, Carmen, Sonia, Esme, and I were sitting at a table in the improvised third-floor library, surrounded by stacks of typed and handwritten poems. Esme's cover was nearly done, and we'd settled on the fonts we wanted to use and how we wanted to arrange the poems in the collection (by topic rather than by author). But before we could go any farther, I explained, we had to make final decisions about which poems we'd include in the magazine.

As we read through manuscripts, we sorted them into piles of first, second, and third choices. When a student came across a poem she particularly liked, she'd read it to the group. And when someone found one she didn't like, she expressed that, too. "This shit is so whack, I can't fucking believe it," Esme declared, penciling an "x" on top of one poem.

"Remember," I said, "we agreed to give only constructive criticism. Try to be specific about what it is about the poem that you dislike."

Esme looked confused, so I rephrased the question in her own terms: "Can you say exactly what is so whack about this shit that you can't fucking believe it?" Just as the expletives left my mouth, another teacher, Irma, stepped out of her office, which opened into the area where we were sitting. She paused, looked around the table at each student in turn, and raised her eyebrows at me, before she walked past.

When Irma was out of sight, the girls exchanged looks with one another. "The teacher got busted," Crystelle whispered to Esme, and they all broke out laughing.

"Okay, back to work," I said.

A few minutes later, one of Crystelle's poems came to the top of Carmen's pile. Crystelle wore her clothes so tight that her breasts were always on display and the top button of her pants was usually left open. She wore large hoop earrings with her name written in cursive across the diameter, a series of thickly braided gold chains around her neck, and wide leather belts that seemed to weigh down her hips the way a cop's holster would. Her eyes seemed to be pleading, even when everything else about her was on the offensive. "Here's a phat poem," Carmen said, smiling at Crystelle. She read it out loud.

When Carmen was finished I agreed. "It is a very strong poem, but I have a concern."

"What's wrong, Miss, you don't like my poem?" Crystelle asked.

"It's a very honest poem," I said, choosing my words carefully. In the poem, Crystelle described her lover in great detail, right down to his "sagging balls." But I wouldn't address that at the moment. "I'm concerned that the description of the subject's 'chinky eyes' is going to offend people."

Crystelle grabbed the paper from Carmen and squinted at her words. She shook her head and said, "There's nothing wrong with that!"

"*Chink* is a derogatory—a mean—way of describing Chinese people," I said.

"No, no, Miss, I just meant his eyes are like…" She lifted her fingers to the corners of her own eyes and stretched them out to create stereotypical Asian features.

"I know that, and I know you don't mean any offense, but *chink* is a word like…"

"Spic," Suleika said, saving me from having to say the word to a group of Puerto Rican girls.

"That shit doesn't bother me," Crystelle said. "I say *spic*. I'm proud of who I am."

"But what if I said it?"

"Go ahead, say it. That don't bother me."

"That's because you know me and you know that I respect you. But if a Chinese person were to pick up a copy of our book, he or she wouldn't know you and they wouldn't know that you didn't mean any disrespect."

Crystelle sucked in her breath and cocked her head at me. "This is my poem and it's my words. I just meant slitty eyes." She pushed away from the table. "I'm going to fight you, Miss," she said and stomped away.

I watched her back recede as she strode down the hall, hips and shoulders swaying with even more than her customary swagger. I didn't know what to do now. I hadn't meant to censor her. I was even willing to overlook the saggy balls—but I couldn't allow a potentially racist comment to appear in our book. I'd hoped to be able to make Crystelle understand this; I'd hoped we could talk it out. But now I wasn't sure that would be possible.

"She's right, our poems are from the heart, we should leave them the way they are," Carmen said.

"Yeah," Luz echoed.

"But we gotta show respect, too," Suleika countered.

"Let's think this one over," I said. "We'll put our decision on hold and keep looking at the rest of the poems."

We got back to the business of reading poem after poem and ranking each one with a number 1, 2, or 3. Luz stopped at a poem one student had written about going through the foster care system. "This one's gonna make everyone cry," she announced. She read it out loud, and the students nodded silently when she finished.

"That was straight up," Suleika said quietly.

Sonia found a poem in Spanish that she liked and read it out loud. Soon almost every poem had found its way into one of the piles, and I commended the students on their hard work.

Just as we were about to call it a day, Crystelle approached from the far end of the hall. She was holding something large in her hand. As she got closer, I could see that it was a hardcover book. She came right up to me and held it in front of my face.

"See," she said, "I'm going to fight you."

By now the book was so close I couldn't read the title. I took a step back and she dropped it on the table. The heavy thunk it made as it landed sent an alarm up my spine. I looked down and saw what it was. Crystelle snapped the dictionary open to a page she'd marked with a Post-it note, and began to read aloud:

"Chink. A crack, cleft, or fissure," she said, pronouncing each word carefully. "A narrow opening." She slammed the book shut and pushed it toward me.

I looked up at Crystelle, who rolled her shoulders back and cocked her head to the side, waiting.

The smile of smug self-satisfaction on her face was so endearing, I didn't want to respond, but I had to. "We'll still have to decide how to handle the poem." I opened the dictionary to the page she had marked. The third definition of the word addressed the slight to Chinese people, I pointed out. "But," I said, "I really like the way you fought me. That was great."

Crystelle nodded. "I gotta go," she said. I looked at my watch.

"Yes, we're done for today." I gathered up the papers. "Good work, ladies," I said as they dispersed down the hall, with Crystelle, in full swagger, leading the way.

Thirteen Different Ways to Look at Me[45]

I am like a dark shadow when
passing by you, you see a person with
two eyes that cry. And in silence, I
suffer. You may look at me as
something precious but that's not how I
feel. I am like a closed capsule, dying
slowly and slowly. Anxious for someone
to find me. I am like rain, non-stop and
clear. Just imagine my flowing tears. I
am like an angel with broken wings.
Desperate to go to heaven so I cannot
feel no more pain. I am like a dead rose
wanting to be alive. Anxious to be able
to breathe again. I am like the color red,
the color of blood pouring out of my
broken heart.

CHAPTER NINE

CHESTER AND DAISY

WALKING THE DOG ON A SATURDAY MORNING, I noticed the forsythia and daffodils had bloomed, tinting the world with a cheerful yellow. One of my favorite things about my neighborhood was that I could choose from among countless routes when setting out to take a walk. But that morning I realized that I no longer considered any option but one. As had become my habit, I walked to the end of my block, where I followed a path through a small patch of woods, emerging at the neighborhood elementary school. From there I walked past small brick houses, ranches and capes, and then a few blocks later entered a neighborhood of grand Tudors and Victorians.

I slowed in front of a beige stucco house with dark wood trim. It was a well-kept gracious home, spread happily on a neatly mowed lawn in a tidy neighborhood that seemed to be trying to live up to the sophisticated names of the streets that bisected it, like Madison Avenue and Irving Place.

This, I'd learned, was the house Mrs. Towne had built for her son, Chester, and his wife, Daisy. Chester and Daisy met in Portland and married in 1911, two years after Chester graduated from Lehigh University. The couple settled in Holyoke, and Chester became managing editor of *Nautilus*. Mrs. Towne, whose father had built a house to her specifications when she was a new bride in Portland, did the same for her son. She purchased the corner lot in May of 1914, the month Chester turned thirty. A year later, Chester and Daisy moved into their new home, where they would raise two daughters.

On one of my increasingly frequent walks past the house, the current owner, a newlywed herself, asked me to wait while she retrieved a torn photograph she'd found under the floorboards during a recent renovation. It was a yellowing portrait of one of Chester's daughters as a toddler, posing outdoors. By now she and several other neighbors knew of me and my interest in Chester and his family. On another of my walks, an elderly woman who lived next door invited me into her cool, dark living room to reminisce about her former neighbor. She described Chester as an absentminded character who drove a Tin Lizzy, had a passion for golf, and had no idea about how to maintain his property. He had gone so far as to ask her late husband to trim *his* hedges, she'd exclaimed.

On this day I continued on my route, heading a few blocks farther south to the street where Chester's sister, Catherine, had lived. Catherine's house, which sits on a narrow lot on a block where homes are packed closely together, looked as if it were once delightful, with its Victorian turrets and wraparound porch. In contrast to Chester's, Catherine's former house was now in poor repair. The paint was peeling and there were missing panes of glass in the upper-story windows. The gardens around back, which I'd viewed one day when I stopped and asked the woman who now tended them if she knew anything of the former inhabitants of her house, were wild and overgrown.

I didn't know as much about Catherine, the older of Towne's two children. From municipal records and old newspaper clippings, I learned that in 1904 she'd married Edward Lincoln Twing, who worked in insurance. They lived in an apartment down the street from the Townes for several years, then moved a couple of times before settling into the house on Fairfield Street with their then fourteen year-old son, Garrison, and one-year-old daughter, Elizabeth, whom I had come to know as Betsy. Maybe because Catherine didn't work for her mother, as Chester had, and therefore was a less public person, I found far less information about her than I had about Chester. There was a detailed description in the local newspaper of Catherine's wedding, including her march to the altar, which was covered in pink roses and peonies, to the strains of Wagner's "Lohengrin." I also found an anecdote about her in the *Nautilus*, in which Towne described hosting a housewarming party for her staff at the house on Cabot Street, during which Catherine was scandalized because her mother had called the party a "house warming tea" and yet no tea was served. ("... Everybody asked for [hot] chocolate," Towne wrote in defense of this eccentricity.)

These two houses, I thought, still seemed to reflect their former tenants' personalities. Chester had been a dutiful son who stayed by his mother's side. He worked for her magazine nearly all his life, starting when, at fifteen, he helped her prepare the first edition of *Nautilus* to be mailed, and then delivered the magazines, which he carried in a sack slung over his shoulder, by bicycle to the post office. In addition to serving as *Nautilus's* managing editor, he helped his mother with her political campaigns, and chronicled her successes in articles he wrote for *Nautilus*. His house was the well-tended, respectable-looking one.

On the other hand, I had only a ghostly image of Catherine. Even my conversations with her daughter, Betsy, netted little information about her. I did learn that she nearly died of toxemia, or pregnancy-induced hypertension, during Betsy's birth. One of the few memories of her mother Betsy shared with me was of Catherine receiving word that her father, Mrs. Towne's first husband, had died. The call came during dinner and Catherine burst into tears when she heard the news. But for the most part Betsy avoided talking about her mother, and when I probed, she tended to shift the conversation back to her grandmother. Catherine's house had a neglected air about it.

After I'd walked the dog past Catherine's house, he trotted toward the corner and turned back in the direction of home. Next time, I promised him, we could take another route.

But days later, my interest in Towne's children was again revived. I was reading a local weekly while eating my lunch. Despite the fact that other newspapers were carrying front-page stories about the ailing stock market and budget cuts to state and federal programs, this paper led with a three-column wedding announcement, as it did nearly every week. Inside, a headline caught my eye. It was a story about "Chester and Daisy." Chester and Daisy, as in the names of Towne's son and his wife, I thought. With so many local history buffs in Holyoke, I wondered if the article might be about Towne's family. Excited, I read on.

The story was by Rita Strong, who writes a chatty news-around-town column. This one turned out to be about how the Marian Center, a retirement home for nuns on Route 5, had acquired two new residents: parakeets named Chester and Daisy. At first I was disappointed. This wasn't a local history story, after all. Or was it?

The fact that the birds were named Chester and Daisy couldn't be mere coincidence, I thought. Maybe the person who had chosen the names for the birds had known Chester and Daisy Struble. And if she had, maybe she could give me information about Mrs. Towne and her family. The birds were in Holyoke, in a nursing home inhabited by elderly women. It wasn't altogether crazy to think that maybe someone there had known Chester and Daisy, was it? I thought about a writing teacher I'd once had who told me that when you're researching a topic, material seems to land on your doorstep as if by magic. I was now sure the Chester and Daisy story had been just such an offering.

After work that day all I wanted to do was head to the nursing home and find out more. But I'd made a commitment to attend an art opening featuring a friend's work and I also had to go grocery shopping and cook dinner for my daughter and partner. When dinner was over, I snuck a look at the clock, but it was too late to drive to the Marian Center.

The next day's schedule was equally unpromising. I had to go to work, and then attend a meeting for parents at my daughter's ballet school. There would be no time to visit the parakeets—unless I left work a little early, headed straight to the Marian Center, checked in on Chester and Daisy, asked my question about who named the parakeets, and continued to the dance school meeting.

Settled into my office that morning, I was about to tell Rhonda of my plan when she launched into a story about how her teenage niece, who had been living with her and her son, had run away the night before. She was anxiously checking her messages to see whether there was one from the girl, or the police.

Later, Celia caught me as I was headed up the stairs and asked me to stop by her office to examine some moldering seeds in one of the flowerpots on the windowsill. She was convinced, she told me, that they'd been hexed by William Towne's spirit. The green fuzz in her electric meditation fountain was surely his doing, too, she said. I put her off and rushed to pick up my students' folders, then flew back downstairs to teach my poetry class. Celia, I thought, was getting carried away with this business about William and the mildew curse. It didn't occur to me then that I might also be getting carried away with my growing obsession with Chester and Daisy the parakeets, not to mention with Towne herself.

In class, Luz read another in a growing series of coming-out poems. This time the assignment had been to write using the prompts "I used to be" and "Now I am."

"I used to be with men / but now I love women," Luz's poem began. The other students in the class had gotten into the habit of praising Luz's courage when she read a poem about her newly discovered sexuality. I was impressed that she was sharing so much in class after months of total silence.

When my last class ended, I'd intended to dart back up to my office, gather my things, and sneak out to the retirement home. I felt a little guilty because I had set aside that time to proofread the manuscript for *Nautilus II*, which was nearly ready to go to the printer. But I couldn't seem to carry out my plan.

Just as I reached the stairs, Rhonda called out to me. "Come to Celia's office; I'm using her computer to print out the cover for *Nautilus II*," she said. Unlike the computer in our office, Celia's computer was loaded with publishing software *and* was connected to a color printer. "It'll just take a minute," she added when I didn't answer right away.

I checked my watch. If I left in the next fifteen minutes I might still be able to carry out my mission. Besides, Rhonda clearly needed something to take her mind off the fact that she'd still had no word from her niece. I followed her to Celia's office.

When we walked inside, Celia was sitting at her desk. "I'm glad you came," she told me. "I want to show you the evidence that William's been up to his tricks." We explained Celia's theory to Rhonda, who pulled the door shut behind her. We examined the slightly fuzzy soil in her flowerpot and the mold growing in her electric fountain. "I don't think it means anything," Rhonda said, sitting down at the computer.

Celia shrugged and sat in one of the chairs students sit in when they come to her office to tell her their problems. "This will just take a minute," Rhonda said, as she clicked open the publishing program on Celia's computer.

"Nothing just takes a minute with that computer. Maybe William's hexed it, too," Celia laughed.

I silently begged William, if his spirit really was in the room, to hurry the computer along so I could investigate the Chester and Daisy situation. But confirming my own theory that his spirit had long since vacated that office, Celia began talking about a rumor we'd all heard, that the budget cuts meant the center had received less grant money for the coming school year, and some staff members would not be rehired. Rhonda got distracted from her mission and became fully engrossed in the issue of budget cuts, worrying that on top of all of her other problems, she would lose her job. By now she seemed to have forgotten what she was there for, no longer even glancing toward the computer.

I was tempted to lean over and press "Print" so we could view the cover and I could be off for the day.

Finally, at three-thirty, I made it out the door. I drove straight to the Marian Center and up the long, curving driveway. It had begun to rain and I didn't have a hat or an umbrella, so I darted from my car to the front door and entered the lobby dripping wet. I didn't see anyone, so I wandered down an empty corridor until a woman in a nurse's slacks and tunic approached me and asked if I needed help.

"I read the story in this week's paper about the parakeets," I began, as if this were a perfectly reasonable thing to say. The nurse nodded, waiting to see if any more comprehensible introduction would follow. When it was clear that was all I had to offer by way of explanation for my dripping wet presence before her, she nodded and led me upstairs. At the nurses' station on the second floor, she passed me over to a middle-aged woman in comfortable street clothes. "This is the activities director," she told me. She explained to the director that I wanted to see the parakeets.

The director did not seem to find my interest in the birds to be unusual. In fact, she explained, the residents had a tank of tropical fish, too. We could take a look at those later, she explained, as she led me to the birdcages.

There were two separate cages set on end tables amid sofas and lamps and a television set in a homey-looking common room. The separate cages, she explained, were necessitated by the fact that Chester had a history of violence.

"Who named the birds?" I asked, determined not to be distracted by Chester's aberrant behavior. My guide called out to another nurse who was passing by. "She's interested in the birds," she told her friend, and nodded in my direction.

Chester, the other nurse explained, was donated to the center by someone and she didn't know where his name originated. As for Daisy, she had chosen the name herself because Daisy's feathers were the sunshiny yellow of that flower's center.

"So they were given to the center by two separate individuals?" I asked. Both women nodded. The disappointment must have been apparent in my voice, because they exchanged confused looks. "You know," I couldn't help saying, "there was a couple living in Holyoke from 1911 until the early '60s named Chester and Daisy." The women nodded, waiting for more. "It's an interesting coincidence, isn't it?" I said. They nodded, looking equally unconvinced.

"Would you like to see the fish?" my guide asked.

"Actually," I said, "I'd better go."

I found my way downstairs and to the main entrance on my own. As I drove through the rain to my daughter's dance school I recalled reading that Elizabeth Towne had been a woman who took over every room she entered. I began to feel she was taking over my imagination as well. If I wasn't careful, I chided myself, I, too, would become convinced that Celia's mold problem had been brought on by the ghost of William Towne.

That week I called Betsy to tell her the *Nautilus II* poetry journal was almost complete. I told her I'd like to dedicate the book to her grandmother and that I wondered what she thought of that. "It would be just lovely," she said.

Then I told Betsy I'd come across an advertisement in an old *Nautilus* about a book Elizabeth Towne had written with Catherine, Betsy's mother. "You haven't told me much about your mother," I said. "I didn't know she wrote a book."

Betsy took a deep breath. "Well, you see," she said, "my mother was very sick. She was in hospitals for most of my life. I didn't know her very well myself."

"I'm so sorry. What did she have?" I asked.

"She had a nervous breakdown," Betsy said.

"A nervous breakdown?" I asked. "Had something traumatic happened? What caused it?"

"You'd have to ask a psychiatrist that," Betsy said. She went on to explain that her father, Edward, had suffered from mental illness, too. They were institutionalized, one after the other, about a year apart.

When Betsy was twelve, after her father was hospitalized, she was sent away to boarding school. This explained her silence on the subject of her parents, and the fact that she knew so little about her grandmother. It also gave me a new perspective on some of the bits and pieces I'd been trying to connect in Elizabeth Towne's story.

———

Elizabeth sat on her bed with little Catherine cuddled at her side. The baby, meanwhile, dozed in his cradle within reach of her arms. Elizabeth knew that rather than turn another page of the book she had propped on her lap, she should be in the kitchen preparing supper for her husband, Joseph, who would arrive in just two hours' time. Yesterday she had been mindful of getting things done properly. She had stuck almost to the minute to the timetable she had laid out for herself, because she determined once and for all that she would master the art of housekeeping.

Elizabeth gave birth to Catherine in 1883, the same year the book *American Nervousness*, in which George Beard blamed modern civilization for an overall degeneration of the nerves of American people, was published. Towne felt herself slipping into Beard's diagnosis. When she was not quite eighteen years old, and with a husband and baby to care for, Towne began to have "dizzy spells and heart failures and bilious spells." Insanity, she feared, would follow.[46]

It wasn't motherhood alone, however, that strained her mental reserves. The daughter of one of Oregon's earliest pioneers and the oldest of four, Elizabeth knew how to care for children. She had left school for the first time at age nine, when a yellow fever epidemic closed it down. When the other students returned, she stayed behind. Her mother had fallen victim to the fever and died giving birth to Elizabeth's youngest sister.

Left to care for her siblings, Elizabeth didn't let her responsibilities interfere with her fun. She would swing from the branch of a tree while her baby sister slept in a basket. And as Elizabeth dropped to the ground to chase her brother and her other sister through the meadow, she would scoop the baby up into her arms as easily as if she were a ball to play with, and continue to run.

Although her father said she'd have to return to school, Elizabeth could see no reason to do so. She'd learned more out of the classroom than in. Outside of school she had learned to dig holes, climb trees, hammer nails, mend fences, and fashion pies out of mud and play-houses out of scrap wood. From spending time at her father's lumber mill, she learned politics from the men's conversations and observed the way the trunk of a grand tree can be transformed into clean, pale two-by-fours. At home, she read incessantly, making her way through the pile of *Harper's* magazines her father had stowed in the closet under the stairs, and she studied her Bible with equal enthusiasm. As for what she learned in school, years later she'd say she couldn't name a thing.

Even after her father insisted Elizabeth and her siblings return to school, she remained interested in life beyond the classroom. She went out dancing every night, coming home after midnight. She'd drop into bed and fall into a dead sleep with her legs aching and her mind still twirling.

At age fourteen, she approached her marriage to Joseph Holt Struble with characteristic energy and enthusiasm. She joked that she hadn't left school—she'd entered Home University. Elizabeth thought keeping house might be one more pleasant lesson to learn. And any-way, her new mother-in-law was there to help.

Only after she and Joseph and their two babies had finally moved into their own house did the crushing reality of her new life descend upon her. It was now for her alone to run the house; the house that she herself had designed and her father had built to her desires (be careful what you wish for, she would remind herself as she tallied up the square footage of floorboards that had to be swept and the number of tables and shelves that had to be dusted). Now she realized with a great shock that she was not mentally equipped to handle the repetitive and con-stant tasks that go into housekeeping.

So she escaped into her novels. She would keep reading and hope that the children would not wake until she got to the end of the story she held in her hands. And when one of those precious angels opened his eyes and wailed, just as she was coming to the climax of a chapter,

Elizabeth would be horrified at the impatient anger she felt rising inside her. Surely no mother on earth was as cruel as she was to think the thoughts she did at moments like that—and all because of a silly book.

She closed the volume mid-sentence and vowed to stop reading altogether if she couldn't pick up and put down a novel without all of this emotion. Not to mention the fact that because of her reading, she had neglected her housework. The trunk of clothes to be sewn was about to spill over again, despite her promise to herself that this very morning she would stitch away until every buttonhole and hem had been repaired. But now, here she was, and the dinner was still uncooked, and the children were yet unwashed, and Joseph would be home, and ...

Elizabeth felt her nerves crackling. But she would not allow her inner demons to triumph. To go insane was ignominious, she told herself. It was always the villains in her books who went insane. She made up her mind then to heal herself of her tempers and her worrying.

Her first attempt at a homegrown approach to staying mentally fit resembled the plan of a disciplinarian who is trying to keep an unruly child in check. Each time her disobedient mind began to race out of control, she would sit herself down in a chair beside the sink and there she would stay until she could quit trembling and work quietly.[47]

When she finally discovered it, New Thought gave her the structure she needed to stave off the encroaching madness she feared. She practiced meditation and trained herself to obey the "godlike" in her consciousness rather than the wild demons.

By practicing New Thought principles with the determination of an athlete preparing for a marathon or an Everest climb, Towne found a way to train her wild mind into orderly submission. New Thought would, paradoxically, also legitimize her eccentricities. It was, after all, an incorporeal voice that would prod her to publish *Nautilus* to begin with, but within the structure of New Thought, listening to such voices was honored. Towne would go on to use her story of mental healing as an inspiration to others who were consumed by worry and nervousness. If she could cure her mental dis-ease, she argued, her readers could certainly cure everything from eyestrain to chronic headaches and the common cold.

Her daughter, I now knew, would not be as lucky. I began to won-der if that was why, other than a few mentions of Catherine in early editions of *Nautilus* and the publication in 1909 of the book they coau-thored, there was little mention of her in any of Towne's published essays and autobiographical writings. Perhaps Elizabeth saw in Catherine the mental defeat she had so feared in herself.

With little else to go on, I set out to search for hints about their relationship in the book they'd co written, *When Is Your Birthday?*, which was written when Catherine was twenty-eight years old, eighteen years before she was committed to a mental hospital for the first time. I bought a copy on eBay and eagerly turned its brittle pages. But the book offered no obvious clues. It turned out to be little more than a glorified horoscope guide, describing each sign, its characteristic traits, and famous New Thought leaders who had been born under it.

I decided, however, that one might read the astrological descrip-tions of each of the author's sun signs as biographies in miniature. Of Taurus, Towne's birth sign, the authors wrote: "People born in this sign are fearless, self-reliant, careful, plodding, inquisitive, curious and sometimes meddlesome ... good business executives ... make splendid healers or physicians and are leaders of reforms, or political move-ments ... [are prone to] morbid mental conditions..."[48]

Of Gemini, Catherine's sign, they wrote: "Changeable and lack concentration. They want to do too many things at a time, and are also apt to take the cares of life too much to heart. Continually borrowing trouble... Through being restless, impatient, anxious, nervous and dis-contented these people lose their health. The diseases most apt to affect them are...nervous diseases and nervous prostration."[49]

Catherine died of heart disease, at age eighty-one, in a state hos-pital for the mentally insane.

———

I had no time to think about Mrs. Towne, Chester, Daisy, or Catherine in the next couple of weeks. *Nautilus II* was about to be pub-lished, and we had a reading and signing planned for the following Wednesday. The printer was supposed to have returned the proofs to me by now, but there had been a delay. I complained to Rhonda that I was afraid the magazine would not be ready on time and I couldn't bear the thought of Wednesday arriving with no *Nautilus II* to celebrate. I'd sent press releases to all of the area newspapers and radio and television stations, and I'd reserved the auditorium in the Wistariahurst Museum, a nineteenth-century mansion down the block from The Care Center, for the event. Any more delays and we'd have a beautifully appointed room full of supporters and eager journalists and no magazine to show. Not to mention the fact that I would have set the students up for one more disappointment. I was spinning these possibilities out for Rhonda as we sat in our office one afternoon.

"Don't worry," Rhonda reassured me. "Mrs. Towne won't let that happen."

On the morning of the reading, I smiled, remembering what Rhonda had said, as I carried a carton of copies of *Nautilus II* from my car past the two marble lions that guarded the museum's entrance. Rhonda helped set up a table for refreshments in the lobby, and we arranged folding chairs in rows in the auditorium. Soon those chairs were filled with students and staff from the center, the editor of a local Spanish-language newspaper, a reporter from the city's paper, and Devon, who had taken an hour off from his job in the History Room to see what we had come up with.

As I stood at the podium, ready to welcome the crowd, I noticed Sylvie, Gloria, and Latisha sitting in the front row. Although we hadn't had any more confrontations, neither had Latisha let her wall of defenses down for me. She had recently found out that she'd passed the GED, so this would be one of the last times I would see her. Marta had come for the reading, even though she was no longer officially enrolled in the school. She'd gotten one part-time job after another, keeping each for a few weeks before she had to quit because of car trouble, her grandfather's illnesses, or her daughter's troubles at preschool. She still was hoping, in spite of all of this, to start classes at the community college in the fall. Esme was out on maternity leave. I'd left a message reminding her about the reading with an older woman who answered her phone, probably her mother or grandmother. She didn't seem to understand much English and I'd meant to call back a few days later in the hopes of speaking to Esme directly, but with the chaos of publishing the magazine, I'd never gotten around to it. Now, as we were about to begin the reading and there was no sign of her in the hall, I was sorry I hadn't tried harder.

I introduced the reading by giving a brief history of Elizabeth Towne, including the reason we'd named our journal after the one she had published. Then I called the first reader to the podium. "Breathe," I whispered, as Luz approached the microphone. She read her pre-coming-out poem that began:

> I am like a dark shadow when
> passing by you, you see a person with
> two eyes that cry. And in silence, I
> suffer...

When she finished, the crowd burst into applause, and knowing that her suffering was now over, I felt exultant.

Desiree, who'd returned to class just weeks before, cried while reading a poem about the beauty of her father's hands. Rosa at the last minute got stage fright and refused to read her piece about a friend who had died. Then Carmen took the stage to read her poem. Carmen had a lot in common with Mrs. Towne, I thought. She, too, had dropped out of school at age fourteen and had two children before her eighteenth birthday. Her poem was called "Forgive Me," a plaintive, straightforward piece that lacked any of the metaphors or figurative language I tried to coax out of my students. But Carmen had remembered the most important rule of our poetry classes: to tell her particular truth the way she saw it. And as it turned out, her poem was the one the newspapers would quote and the audience would sigh and clap for.

> Mom, forgive me.
> I know I did lots of stuff wrong.
> I tried to do stuff right.
> But it was hard.
> Now I am grown
> Have two kids
> and always think
> I don't want that to happen to me.

I wish I could go back in the days
and say Mom
Forgive Me.
Mom what I did was wrong
I know it wasn't right
I did not listen and also did not go to school
I wish I listened to every word that came out of your mouth.
I know I got you through stuff
that I wish you never went through.
If I would have listened I would've never been here.
So please, please and please forgive me.[50]

Just as I was getting ready to thank everyone for coming to our event, Esme walked in, carrying an infant. I waved her up to the stage. She handed the baby to one of the counselors and made her way to the podium to deliver her poem.

When the reading was over, I handed the students colorful gel pens I'd bought at the dollar store and told them it was customary for authors to sign copies of their books. They took their places in a row of chairs that had been arranged in the front of the auditorium, and I invited members of the audience to come up to have their books signed.

"You can just write your name, or you can write a little message," I coached the poets. One by one, teachers, reporters, and a handful of people from the community who had read about the event in the newspaper lined up. Rhonda and I joined them. "If Mrs. Towne is watching this, she's delighted," Rhonda whispered to me. I looked down the row of students, each bent studiously over someone else's journal, pen in hand. For a moment I indulged in the pure joy of the moment.

Then, seeing Latisha, with her characteristically moody expression, I almost regretted having joined the line for signatures. I feared I was setting myself up for a parting insult from her. I still didn't feel comfortable in her presence and was secretly relieved on those days she was absent. I made an excuse to leave and asked Esme, who was penning her name with gusto, to "just pass my book along when you're done."

I checked in with the reporters to make sure they had all the information they needed, then began to gather up the books that hadn't been sold and pack them back into their boxes. When everyone else had gone, I took a moment to thank all of the poets for their good work and their courage in reading their poems to the public. "I can't tell you how proud I am of all of you today," I said. We gave ourselves a big round of applause and filed out of the museum, down the street, and back to class.

I carried my copy of *Nautilus II*, feeling the way I had when I carried my students' poetry folders back to my office. I was flushed with the excitement of anticipation. But in this case, my ebullient mood was also tinged with apprehension. I feared what Latisha might have written. Probably just her name, I told myself. But would she have taken this chance to have the last word? I sat at my desk and opened the book. There were signatures in glittery green, pink, and purple ink. Luz's filigreed script spread down one side of the title page, Jazmin's signature, just below it, was self-conscious in the style of most teenagers', Suleika's was self-possessed and upright. Someone added a "Good Luck," and another a "Thank You." Carmen had written, "Thank you for forcing me to write poetry. Now I see how far it can take me." I smiled at that.

I quickly flipped through the rest of the pages to find the place where Latisha had signed. "Thanks," she had written, "you never gave up."

———

I hadn't been back to the library since before the incident with Chester and Daisy, the parakeets. The birds had become a symbol to me of my obsession with Elizabeth Towne's life. I decided I had learned enough about her and that it was time to reclaim my imagination. But when I'd seen Devon at the *Nautilus II* reading, he had insisted that I come by to visit. "I dug up a few things you might be interested in," he'd said.

When I came in later that week, I noticed that the renovation of the children's section of the library had finally been completed. Formerly on the basement level, the room had been relocated to the ground floor so that now the area that had been reserved for quiet reading was cheerfully furnished and decorated with colorful posters proclaiming the joys of reading. I walked past the rows of new bookshelves and up the broad staircase to the History Room, where Devon greeted me with a smile.

"When we were digging around in the basement during the renovation, we found some interesting things," he told me. He led me to the stacks of books by local authors, where months ago we had looked for works by Mrs. Towne and found nothing. Devon swept his hand along two large bookcases. They were now filled with leather-bound copies of *Nautilus*, ranging from 1907 to 1951. I was elated. I picked them up one by one and cradled each in my hands.

Mrs. Towne just won't let me go, I thought as I fingered the brittle binding of a volume from 1911. I practically danced back to the table so I could begin to read.

I was overwhelmed by the bounty. I read a little bit from one issue, then skipped ahead ten years, then back seven. I would never be able to read all of them, so I decided to check momentous years: the year the house burned down, the year she marched for women's suffrage in Boston, the years of each of her runs for public office.

Devon stopped at my table to check on my progress. "Finding anything good?" he asked, as he always did. I nodded with vigor. How could I possibly express in words just how good it was to be hearing Mrs. Towne's voice across the bounds of time—to be subsumed by the volume of her chatter?

I'd meant for this to be a quick trip, just to say hello to Devon. But already an hour and a half had passed. Reluctantly, I put the volume I'd been reading back on the shelf. I'd been wearing a pair of khaki pants and a light green jacket over my white T-shirt. I looked down now to see that my jacket was smudged with reddish-brown streaks. For a moment my heart froze. Was I bleeding? I held up my hands and examined them. They were covered in dull red smudges, too. It took me a moment to realize it was not dried blood but the dust from the deteriorating leather binding of the books I'd been handling.

I liked to think the books *were* bleeding. As if life were pouring out of them. As if they had overcome the doom of obscurity and forgetfulness, the only real death, and had burst back to life.

When I returned to the center, Carmen, the secretary, stopped me before I could walk past the front office. "You have a phone message," she said, and handed me a square of pink paper. It was from an older woman who as a child had known Mrs. Towne. She'd read about the new *Nautilus* and wanted to talk to me.

That night I had a dream in which I was at a banquet table, seated among dignitaries from Holyoke. A man handed me a large, antique, leather-bound book. I flipped through the pages and found Elizabeth Towne's name in it. I was thrilled. He asked me: "Why are you so interested in her?"

I still didn't have an answer. But when I woke, I wondered if it wasn't so much that I was interested in Mrs. Towne as that she was interested in me. Perhaps her spirit *was* in my office, the room I now knew she had called the Campfire Club Room, and where she hosted lectures and meetings and groups of like-minded women and men. Perhaps she saw that I needed the companionship of a like-minded woman myself, if I were to feel comfortable in her home.

THROUGH MY WINDOW I SEE[51]

The neighbor from across,
he always wears the same outfit.
Black jeans and of course a black jeans jacket.
Through this window I see
Margarita at 6 a.m. digging in the Dumpster.
I see her husband repeat the same at nighttime.
I see Margarita's neighbor who only goes to his house to get something, and then leaves. Never stays in his house.
I see the perfect star and the perfect moon, right next to the star.
I see the cable guy who lives in the same court leave the lights on in his car.
I see myself seeing all of this.
I see myself looking out my window.

CHAPTER TEN

OUR LITTLE "WELL DONE"

IN ITS DAY, MRS. TOWNE'S HOUSE WAS NICKNAMED the "High School Annex" because of the numbers of young women employed there (more than seventy local girls in a ten-year span, and a couple dozen at any given time), and also because of Towne's self-appointed mission to help her employees improve themselves.

These workers (secretaries, stenographers, and housekeepers) became a kind of family. The Townes hosted picnics for their employees and made holiday postcards featuring group photographs of the office staff posed on the front steps and sent them out to subscribers. Towne took an interest in her employees' social lives, pending nuptials, and educational plans.

Mrs. Towne ministered lessons to her employees as well. When, for example, one housekeeper repeatedly replaced books on the shelves upside down, Towne tried reminding, then scolding her. But when the books kept appearing wrong side up, she called the young woman into her office, closed the door, and faced her with a stern look. "I've been considering this for some time now," she said, "and it is borne in upon me that I have a duty in the matter which I must not shirk. Probably the city authorities ought to be notified," she went on, watching as the girl's eyes began to grow wide with alarm. "It is against the public good, you know, for people to be illiterate," Towne continued. "I think it really is my duty to see that you learn to read."

"But I *can* read," the housekeeper protested.

"Surely you *can't*," Towne replied, "because if you could, then you wouldn't have done *that*," she said, pointing to a half dozen books that were set wrong in the case. The housekeeper burst into laughing, and as Towne relates the story, the books were aligned tidily ever after.

Another time she replaced an oft-ignored sign that read, "Please close the door," with another that read, "I am treating the rats to catch the girls who leave this door open!!!" The latter, she found, did the trick.[52]

"Our office supplies schooling as well as work," Towne was quoted as saying in a 1912 newspaper article. "We teach the best methods we know for doing all kinds of work, believing that responsibilities honestly discharged and all work efficiently and good-willingly done make for character, and character makes for success and happiness and health." She went on, "We 'graduate' our workers just as a school does—when a helper reaches the place where she no longer grows by doing our work, we are glad to present her with our little 'Well done,' as a sort of diploma and pass her on to new opportunities."

I thought of Mrs. Towne and her little "well dones" as the mayor of Holyoke took the podium during The Care Center's graduation ceremony that June.

"This is really a tribute to overcoming obstacles," he was saying, as he looked out over rows of graduates in their white satiny robes, each fanning herself with a folded program of the day's events that had been photocopied onto marbled yellow paper. In addition to being hot, the room was loud. Parents and grandparents held babies in their laps, and children were crying from boredom and discomfort. The students who were not graduating that day were the most attentive, dreaming, I supposed, that they might be among those draped in white next year. For now, they wore tube tops, backless or shoulder-less shirts, lollipop red shorts or hip hugger pants, fringed belts, and chunky high-heeled shoes. Pregnant bellies burst from tight denim dresses, midriff T-shirts, and floral print blouses. Nearly every head was carefully coifed: hair was braided, relaxed, straightened, extended, or exquisitely curled.

As Mayor Sullivan, a man with a friendly Irish face and the build of a teddy bear, continued with his talk, I looked out on the graduates. Their frightened faces, like a constellation of stunned moons, glowed beneath the vaulted ceiling. Under some of those robes, nested in pregnant bellies, new lives curled like question marks—easy enough to ignore for the moment, so their mothers could stand and take their certificates feigning brave certainty of something better.

I saw Esme reach up to adjust her mortarboard, and I remembered how she once told me she had always dreamed of going to her high school graduation and her senior prom, but then she got pregnant and gave up on ever experiencing this pomp and circumstance. When I told her she'd get to wear a cap and gown for the center's ceremony, she kept her face blank for a moment, as if she were waiting for me to say I was just joking. But when I reassured her it was true, she said, "Hey, that's phat."

Speaker after speaker rose to address the group. Standing beneath a Puerto Rican and an American flag, they delivered their comments in English and Spanish, quoting everyone from Nelson Mandela to popular singers. The keynote speaker, a health educator who specialized in teaching young people about sexually transmitted diseases, and whom the girls had nicknamed "The Sex Lady," slipped a CD into a player and asked the audience to listen to the lyrics of a song by Yolanda Adams: "Don't be afraid to face the world against all odds. Don't give up. Don't give up."

Ana, in her bright pink pants and tropical-print blouse, took the stage next. "This is a second chance for all of you," she was saying. Ana was the reason we were assembled in that elegant hall, instead of handing out certificates in one of the large classrooms in the center or the basement of a nearby church. Her senior year in high school, Ana had a 4.0 grade point average and had received impressive scores on her SATs. But the administrators at her school in Salinas, Puerto Rico, asked her to stay home on graduation day because she was unmarried and eight months pregnant. It was thanks to her that the center's graduation had all the formality of a traditional high school affair. She didn't want her students to be cheated the way she had been.

As she continued to speak, her eyes took in each student, as if she were taking attendance. Then her gaze fell on Gloria, who, we'd learned the week before, had failed the GED—again. This time she'd missed by only a handful of points. I watched Gloria bite her lip to hold back tears. "I know how hard it is," Ana continued. "You wake up early and get your children ready for school. Then you get yourselves ready for school." Her eyes were locked on Gloria's now. "I don't want any one of you girls to give up." Both she and Gloria stopped trying not to cry. "Do *not* give up. You are going to make it." Ana wiped streams of tears from her cheeks. She repeated what she just said in Spanish, then took her seat. All of the noise in the room was focused into one sound now: applause thundered through the hall.

——

The term *graduation* implies the end of one's studies. *Commencement* means a beginning. I'm not sure which best applies to The Care Center's ceremony. I prefer the word *commencement*, and with it the vision of these young women starting out on new lives—although I know for many, this will be the end, or close to it, of their formal studies.

For me, each graduation *is* an ending. It represents the last time I will see most of the students who receive their certificates. But from time to time I'd run into a former student downtown, and she'd tell me that she still had a poetry book I'd given her and that she and her boyfriend read it together, or that she had a good job—or that she recently lost one. When I ran into Desiree in the lobby of the bank and asked what she'd been up to, she replied flatly, "nothing." I'd see others on the campus of the community college. I'd run into a graduate on High Street and she'd tell me she was working in a day care center. Another would be on her way to a class to train to be a nurse's assistant. Some I wouldn't see, but I'd hear about. Someone would ask me, "Have you heard about Ivy? It's so sad. She's all strung out on crack." One day I'd be picking up a pizza to bring home, and there would be Ruth in a rusted-out silver Ford wearing a red and blue uniform. I'd ask if she'd written anything lately and she'd shake her head. "No time," she'd mumble.

Luz, I heard through one of the counselors, had broken up with her girlfriend and was thinking of reuniting with her baby's father. Marta stopped by to visit often. Last I'd heard she had two jobs, had moved her daughter and grandfather into a bigger apartment, and was off welfare. Latisha got a job as a nurse's assistant. I would run into her downtown years later, and she would smile and tell me she'd written a poem just the night before. "I was angry so it was full of some nasty stuff," she'd say. "I bet it felt good to get it out," I'd reply, as if we were back in class. "It did," she'd admit, laughing this time.

Then there was Esme. Halfway through her first semester at college, she would find out she was pregnant again and drop out.

If graduation were a time of secure and happy endings, or assured bright beginnings, it might be easier for me to once more unpack my tote bag full of volumes of poetry and clean sheets of lined paper and tell the next group of students that I wanted to teach them to express on paper their particular truth the way they see it. Instead, I find my inspiration from a painting that for a long time hung in the second-floor hallway of the center.

It's a seascape, with two coconut trees in the foreground arcing out over a sapphire blue ocean. In it, a boat floats toward the horizon, where an orange ball of a sun sinks out of view. It's a depiction of a dream of some warm and distant place—the ideal of home on the horizon, or a wished-for memory: the blues and greens, the energetic churn of white where the sea meets the sun-warmed shore.

It's a lovely painting that displays no particular talent. Every time I passed it, though, I thought of the student who had made it. Evelyn wore movie-star sunglasses, even indoors, and lots of flashy gold jewelry. She painted her lips with shimmering pink gloss, and she was honest, quiet, and persistent. After three years of trying, she left the center, as many students did, without ever passing the GED.

The boat, floating in the background of her painting, was sketched in pencil, revealing the nubby surface of the unpainted canvas. Evelyn never finished it. Her poetry folder, too, remains in my drawer, where I keep the poems of students who've left and for whom I have no current address.

The art teacher once saw me admiring her painting, and said, "I should let one of the students finish the boat for her."

I nearly shouted my objection. That unpainted swath of canvas has taught me more than anything else could about my job as a teacher. Whether that empty space in an ocean of color represents potential not yet realized or a hope never fulfilled, it speaks the truth. I teach knowing it may never be filled in.

The GED is not a magic fix. Poetry is not a magic fix. Even the cliché, "If I can change just one life," is something I've let go of. It's not my business, I've concluded, to decide who needs to be changed or how. As the poetry teacher at the center, I give each student an hour a week to visit her imagination. That, to me, has become enough of a goal, enough of a justification—a sincere offering.

I'm still learning from Evelyn's painting, still captivated by the raw edge of canvas showing through. The hope of reclaiming the colors. The truth of the painting, poem, or story left unfinished. The courage to admit I don't know how it ends.

Or that it doesn't.

ETERNAL[53]

If I can't be eternal
I'll be the wind
I'll go around the whole
world then come back
If I can't be eternal
I'll be a guardian angel
knowing everything
you do without ever you
finding out.

CHAPTER ELEVEN

I'LL WATCH FOR YOU

THERE WAS A MOMENT, BEFORE SHE FULLY UNDERSTOOD what was happening, when Mrs. Towne was caught between the dream she had just been immersed in, and the shouts to wake up, wake up.

The heat was a splendid surprise—as if all of her unspoken wishes for warmth in that frozen month had been multiplied to a cruel sum and now answered with a thunderous breath.

Wake up, wake up.

She and William plowed through the seamless smoke. They rushed to Mother Towne's room, where it took all four—Elizabeth, William, and both housekeepers—to hoist William's aged mother, who'd been living with them for a time, out of her bed.

The steady heat of the flames thudded like waves of sound. The fire woke every cell and sense to battle, to strive for life against death.

Wake up, wake up.

Fire after fire, it seemed to Elizabeth. Her father's mill going up in flames not one but two times during her childhood. And the house itself, the one that she had played in as a girl, had burned down in the years since she had left it. She remembered the astrologer's warnings when they purchased this house four years earlier. Fiery Mars was ruling the skies that spring, the fortune-teller had said, and she should beware of the flames.

At the time, Towne replied with her own fire: "Whatever way the pugnacious, aggressive, fiery and explosive Mars might exhibit his influence, I will be on deck to make the best of the situation."[54] And then a rumor spread, just a few years back, and she had to answer in print in *Nautilus* that no, her home had not burned. Was the rumor simply premature? Or had the imaginations of her readers, and her own fears, materialized this monster of destruction?

Maybe she'd been dreaming of Mrs. Eddy? The founder of the Christian Science church had died just days before—had Mrs. Towne allowed herself to feel smug in outliving her rival? Were these flames Mrs. Eddy's heated laughter in response?

Wake up, wake up.

What should she try to rescue from this inferno? What precious items should she try to salvage?

"No time," William was yelling. "Run, run."

The January issue of *Nautilus* had just been sent to the printer and so had been saved. The children, grown and on their own, were spared, too. Outside the house, just beyond the lawn, crowds were gathering, open mouths gaping. Their expressions told Elizabeth that this was certainly no dream. No small misfortune, either.

God is here, she told herself, even as her beautiful yard was being transformed into a hellish desert. God is working in and through each person gathered here. Peace within, she coaxed herself.

And here were the neighbors, coming to lift Mother Towne from William's arms. Alive. There they all stood: Elizabeth, William, and both housekeepers crying in one another's arms. All saved. Except for the papers inside. All of her words. Curled and blackened and disappeared.

Elizabeth tried only to be grateful, though. The fire company was there with their hoses. "Save the barn," she shouted. The house is gone, but please, God, save the barn. Inside it were stored the archived issues of her magazine.

Was it the Gurney heater that caused the blaze? Elizabeth tried to roll back the events of that night. They had not been sleeping long; they'd only arrived home at half past eleven. It had been the coldest night that winter, but they had refused to stay inside and carried forth with their plans to attend the theater. They returned tingling with cold, but also warmed by their own righteousness. They had not been prisoners of this interminable winter. They had gone out into the elements, had pushed ahead with their own happiness. And William, William had built up that good and rousing fire to warm them when they returned. As she had closed the door to her room, Elizabeth heard the hiss and gurgle of steam rising in the radiator and she thought of fire, could hear the *siss* of flames against cold air, and told herself to stop that old habit of worry. "I have worried about fire long enough," she told herself and put herself to sleep.

The water came crashing down against what was left of their grand house. And as if time were stopping for their sake—so they could catch up with the grim reality that had overtaken them in their sleep—the water froze where it landed.

"The January *Nautilus* is saved," Elizabeth heard herself telling William. "We must get to work on February."

A cup of hot cocoa was placed in her hands. Blankets were wrapped around her nightgown. The flames warmed her breast while the icy wind slapped her back.

By breakfast time the firemen, walking stiffly in their frozen uniforms, hauled in their hoses. Unable to roll the icy snakes, they simply dragged them behind the truck and back to the station, leaving the glittering wreckage in their wake.

Elizabeth woke the next afternoon in Catherine and Edward's house just down the street. Even with the windows closed tight against the freezing temperatures, Elizabeth was sure she could smell her own house smoldering.

The next afternoon's newspaper reported the arithmetic of her tragedy. It had been a zero-degree night. The blaze broke out at one in the morning. The damage multiplied quickly to create a loss worth $12,000.[55]

It would be an easy, even an understandable choice to slip into depression now. The fire erased five years of renovations and improvements on the house. Just weeks before, she and William had pronounced the job complete, the house in order and to their liking. But depression was no longer an option for Mrs. Towne. Not after all she'd been through. And certainly not with an audience of 31,000 readers watching. Her readers counted on her to exemplify the principles of New Thought.

She remembered again her early years as a mother, with two small babies and not even grown herself. She remembered how she'd nearly lost her sanity trying to make it along the deceptively simple path from morning till night. But she had prevailed. She remembered moving, a dozen or so years back, from one flat to another in the Majestic, a building a ten-minute walk from where she stood now. She had written in an early issue of *Nautilus* that moving need not be drudgery: "It certainly is true that the whole world hastens to get out of the way for the man or woman who knows where he is going. Not only that but the whole world hastens to get him there."

Where were they going now? She knew at once. They would use the insurance money to rebuild the house and make it even more magnificent than before. What were those lines from Holmes's poem, "The Chambered Nautilus"? Of course:

> Year after year beheld the silent toil
> that spread his lustrous coil:
> Still, as the spiral grew,
> He left the past year's dwelling for the new.

On Tuesday, May 16, perhaps as a slightly delayed birthday present for Mrs. Towne, who celebrated her forty-sixth birthday on the eleventh, and less than five months after the fire burned the original residence nearly to the ground, the new cornerstone for her rebuilt home was put in place. This house was even grander than the first, she proclaimed, and had been built with every protection available against future fires.

> ...Stole with soft step its shining archway through,
> Built up its idle door,
> Stretched in his last-found home, and knew the old no more.

Elizabeth Towne continued to publish *Nautilus* from her house on Cabot Street until August 1951, when, citing health issues, she sold the magazine to the Pacific Coast Authority, another New Thought publisher.

She remained in the house for nine more years, her health declining, until, at age ninety, she could only sit in her wheelchair and read a bit each day, or hum the Welsh tunes of her ancestors, which she still recalled from childhood.[56] In February 1960 she entered a local nursing home, and a few months later, at age ninety-five, she died.[57]

Rather than be buried she elected to be cremated, a highly unorthodox practice then, and one which once more, and for the last time, succeeded in raising eyebrows among her neighbors.

—

One day, as spring was easing into summer, I walked out of The Care Center and made my way past two workmen who were examining the porch and stairs. One was nudging a loose piece of cement with the toe of his work boot.

"Looks like we're getting some new steps," I said.

The cars driving by on Cabot Street had their windows rolled down, releasing the beat of reggaeton music into the sun-warmed air. The workmen wore T-shirts, tool belts, and jeans. One had graying hair and a strong build. The other was younger with a ponytail. I was eager to get to my car and put down my tote bag, which was stuffed with Emily Dickinson's collected works, an anthology of Latina poetry, and that day's crop of student poems. But my mind was calculating as quickly as my feet were walking: Cement. Chisels. Workmen. And before I had time to weigh my words, I found myself turning back toward the building.

"Hey, what would it take to remove a cornerstone?" I asked.

"A what?"

"A cornerstone. The one right here on this building. Could you take it out?"

The men exchanged "crazy lady" glances as I walked over to the northwest corner of the house, slipped between the shrubs and the bricks, and pointed to the white stone carved with the competing dates of 1898, when the house was first built, and 1911, when it was rebuilt after the fire. I had recently found an old newspaper story about the reconstruction of the house, in which Towne is quoted as saying that when the house was rebuilt from the ashes she had inserted a time capsule into the cornerstone.

Inside the stone, William and Elizabeth had sealed artifacts of the history of the *Nautilus*. They'd included copies of the magazine, photographs of the Townes and their employees, and an article about the *Nautilus* from the perspective of one of their employees, a Miss Frances Kidnay. Catherine's photograph, on the back of which she was identified as the "Office Angel," was also tucked inside. Each of the homes in which the *Nautilus* had been published was memorialized with a photograph, including the house in Portland where Towne published the first four-page issue, the house on Cabot before it burned, and the house at Maple and Appleton where they'd printed the magazine while their new quarters were being erected. Finally, to finish off the story of *Nautilus*'s evolution, Towne included a sketch of the new dwelling and an article about the fire. Someone threw in a handful of coins before the box was sealed.

"A time capsule?" the younger man asked.

"Maybe there's hidden treasure in there," the other man said.

"I think it's just some old magazines and photographs," I explained. "We'd need Ralph's permission."

Ralph, the landlord, would be unlikely to say yes. From what I'd heard, he already considered The Care Center to be a difficult tenant, with our students who not only painted murals on the interior walls but also irked the neighbors by taking cigarette breaks on any available stoop.

"I'd even pay for it myself," I said.

The older man raised his eyebrows. "I should be seeing Ralph soon," he said.

"Would you ask him?"

He said he would and I thanked him and continued to my car. Maybe, I thought, maybe we could do it.

It had been a long day, and as I drove home my thoughts turned back to my students. Sonia had complained during class that she was tired and couldn't sleep. Couldn't I see the bags under her eyes? she asked me. I suggested she try memorizing a poem and recite it to herself silently as she lay in bed. "It'll relax you and take your mind off your worries," I told her. "Besides," I joked, "you girls always complain that poetry puts you to sleep."

Later, just as I was leaving my office with Rhonda, Gloria had called out to me and asked if I'd remembered to bring her the Emily Dickinson poem she'd been working on translating into Spanish. I gave her a copy and when I got to the first floor, Suleika wanted to know if she could take home one of the poems I'd typed for her. "I want to hang it in my room," she said. I pictured her taping the poem above her bed in the homeless shelter where she was living with her son.

Ebony, meanwhile, had stomped out the door of the school and walked right past me without a word. After disappearing for a couple of months in the winter, Ebony had returned and seemed to be settling in; in fact, she was getting ready to take the GED exam in a few weeks. But that afternoon she was furious because she'd missed the van and would have to walk home. At that moment anger defined her, but just hours before, she'd been telling me how much she loves poetry now, and how she's writing her own book at home.

"Bring it in for our next class," I said. "I'd love to see it."

She shook her head. "I won't be in school for a while. I'm going down to Delaware to see my brother." Her brother was an alcoholic, but Ebony was certain she could save him. "I know he'll listen to me," she told me after I had warned her not to leave school now when she was so close to testing.

"You need to take care of yourself and your baby right now. Your brother will take care of himself," I said. Then a line from a new student's poem came to me. This had been her first day of poetry class, and she had written, "The addicts have no choice. / All of this has been around forever."

Ebony didn't listen to me when I told her she couldn't change her brother. In a way, she was acting like Mrs. Towne—and me: white liberals who want to think that *they* (the politicians, the welfare bureaucrats, the conservative voters, the mayor, the president, the prison guards, the police, the social workers, the drunken brothers ...) will listen to *us*. That we can storm in with our good intentions and make, what else?—a difference.

I never heard back from the workmen about whether they'd asked Ralph about the cornerstone. Nor did I pursue the matter any further. Instead, I imagined what it would be like if we had been able to remove the stone and find Mrs. Towne's time capsule. The workers would sandblast and chisel and slide the cornerstone out, and perhaps a reporter from the local newspaper would be standing in the ring of onlookers, and maybe the old magazines and photographs would be intact. And then I would hold the pages, delicate as a moth's wings, in my hands. I might finally see a picture of Catherine or I might learn one or two new facts to put on the time line I'd created of Mrs. Towne's life, which by now ran to seventeen pages. That would be exciting. Or maybe it would be a disappointment. Certainly it would feel like the end of something. I'd have gotten as close to Mrs. Towne as I could.

Instead of calling Ralph about the cornerstone, I called Yari, one of my first students at the center. I wanted to know how she was faring now that she'd started taking classes at the community college. I wondered if I could stop by her apartment and bring her a copy of *Nautilus II*. She said, "Oh, sure, come and visit. My buzzer is the third from the bottom, there are no names, but I'll watch for you."

Chambered Nautilus

Oliver Wendell Holmes

This is the ship of pearl, which, poets feign,
Sails the unshadowed main,—
The venturous bark that flings
On the sweet summer wind its purpled wings
In gulfs enchanted, where the Siren sings,
And coral reefs lie bare,
Where the cold sea-maids rise to sun their streaming hair.

Its webs of living gauze no more unfurl;
Wrecked is the ship of pearl!
And every chambered cell,
Where its dim dreaming life was wont to dwell,
As the frail tenant shaped his growing shell,
Before thee lies revealed,—
Its irised ceiling rent, its sunless crypt unsealed!

Year after year beheld the silent toil
That spread his lustrous coil;
Still, as the spiral grew,
He left the past year's dwelling for the new,
Stole with soft step its shining archway through,
Built up its idle door,
Stretched in his last-found home, and knew the old no more.

Thanks for the heavenly message brought by thee,
Child of the wandering sea,
Cast from her lap, forlorn!
From thy dead lips a clearer note is born
Than ever Triton blew from wreathèd horn!
While on mine ear it rings,
Through the deep caves of thought I hear a voice that sings:—

Build thee more stately mansions, O my soul,
As the swift seasons roll!
Leave thy low-vaulted past!
Let each new temple, nobler than the last,
Shut thee from heaven with a dome more vast,
Till thou at length art free,
Leaving thine outgrown shell by life's unresting sea!

ENDNOTES

[1] The article students were reading in class was published in
Holyoke: A Weekly Union News Magazine, January 18, 1996, pp. 6–9.
[2] Poem by Care Center student Fantasia Cash.
[3] Poem by Care Center student Evangellyn Bonilla.
[4] Poem by Care Center student Yaritza Figueroa.
[5] Poem by Care Center Student Christia Rosa.
[6] As performed by Saul Williams in the movie *Slam* (Trimark 1998).
[7] U.S. Census Bureau, 2000.
[8] "Juntos Adult Basic Education Collaborative Assets and Needs Report,"
Holyoke, Mass., 2003 (based on U.S. Census and local data).
[9] Laurence Steinberg, *Adolescence* (New York: McGraw Hill, 1996) pp. 396 –
431.
[10] Cynthia Robbins, H. B. Kaplan, and S. S. Martin, "Antecedents of Pregnancy Among Unmarried Adolescents," *Journal of Marriage and the Family,* 47
(3) pp. 567–583.
[11] Poem by Care Center student Erin Rowe.
[12] Poem by Care Center student Evangellyn Bonilla.
[13] I read these words by the famed educator Paulo Freire in a speech given
by Martha S. Jones, delivered at the Graduate School of Arts and Sciences
Commencement, 2000, and printed in *Columbia* magazine, Fall 2003.
[14] Poem by Care Center student Rosalie Castillo.
[15] Poem by Care Center student Claribel Oquendo.
[16] From "Goodbye, Mr. Koch," by Mrs. Wick's class. Kenneth Koch,
Wishes Lies and Dreams: Teaching Children to Write Poetry (New York: Harper
Perennial, 1999), p. 61.
[17] Anthony Gomes, in *Wishes, Lies and Dreams,* p. 144.
[18] Poem by Care Center student Silia Vega.
[19] By Care Center student Monica Colon.
[20] Marcella R. Kelly, "Behind Eternity: Holyoke Women Who Made a
Difference," published for Holyoke's Centennial celebration, 1973, p. 154.
[21] Dr. Raymond C. Barker, ed., *New Thought Bulletin,* from a newspaper article
(January 29, 1945), clipped but unmarked in the Holyoke History Room,
Holyoke Public Library, Holyoke, Mass.
[22] Poem by Care Center student Marilyn Rodriguez.
[23] From a letter reprinted in *Freedom,* December 21,1898, cited in Beryl

Satter, *Each Mind a Kingdom: American Women, Sexual Purity and the New Thought Movement*, 1875–1920, (Los Angeles and London: University of California Press, 1999), note p. 326.

[24] From the New Thought website cornerstone.wwwhubs.com/towne.htm.

[25] Letter from Kay Struble to Jed Mattes, dated May 12, 1978.

[26] Ida Craddock Papers, letter from Elizabeth Towne dated March 13, 1902; and James R. Petersen, *The Century of Sex: Playboy's History of the Sexual Revolution, 1900–1999* (New York: Grove Press, 1999).

[27] Charles Samuel Braden, *Spirits in Rebellion: The Rise and Development of New Thought* (Dallas, Tex.: Southern Methodist University Press, 1984), p. 341.

[28] Braden, p. 338.

[29] Poem by Care Center student Limary Gonzalez.

[30] Poem by Care Center Student Fantasia Cash.

[31] Poem by Care Center Student Syeanna Sepulveda.

[32] *Holyoke Transcript-Telegram*, November 10, 1928, p. 1.

[33] *Holyoke Transcript-Telegram*, October 4, 1927, p. 7; October 5, 1927, p. 8–9.

[34] *Nautilus*, September 1927.

[35] Monroe Billington, "Susanna Madora Salter: First Woman Mayor," *Kansas Historical Quarterlies* (Fall 1954, vol. 21, no. 3), pp. 173–183 at www.kancoll.org/khq/1954/54_3_billington.htm; www.umkc.edu/imc/womenfi.htm.

[36] Ross Anderson, *The Seattle Times*, September 16, 2001, http://seattletimes.nwsource.com/news/local/seattle_history/articles/citys_50_mayors.html.

[37] *Holyoke Transcript-Telegram*, November 30, 1928.

[38] *Holyoke Transcript-Telegram*, December 3, 1928, pp. 18–19.

[39] *Holyoke Transcript-Telegram*, December 5, 1928.

[40] Poem by Care Center student Marta Montalvo.

[41] Poem by Care Center student Betsy Franco.

[42] Poem by Care Center student Betsy Franco.

[43] Ferriss Clay Bailey, *Preachers Without Pulpits: New Thought and the Rise of Therapeutic Self-Help in Progressive Era America* (Nashville, TN, Vanderbilt University Doctoral Dissertation, May 1990), note p. 22; and Satter, p. 226.

[44] Elizabeth Towne, *Elizabeth Towne's Experiences in Self Healing* (Holyoke, MA: The Elizabeth Towne Co., Inc., 1905), p. 46.

[45] Poem by Care Center student Betsy Franco.

[46] *Self Healing*, p. 4.

[47] *Self Healing*, pp. 4–5.

[48] Elizabeth Towne and Catherine Struble Twing, *When Is Your Birthday?* (Holyoke, MA: The Elizabeth Towne Co., Inc., 1919), pp. 31–32.

[49] *When is Your Birthday?* pp. 36–37.

[50] Poem by Care Center student Carmen Cabrera.

[51] Poem by Care Center student Lily Torres.

[52] *Nautilus*, October 1906, p. 40.

[53] Poem by Care Center student Yashira Colon.

[54] *Nautilus*, May 1911, p. 14.

[55] The sum of $12,000 in 1911 is the equivalent of $200,000 of today's dollars, according to a calculation using the Consumer Price Index calculator, http://minneapolisfed.org/Research/data/us/calc/index.cfm.

[56] Letter from Kay Wister to Garrison Struble Twing dated May 9, 1973, and *Holyoke Transcript-Telegram*, May 11, 1955.

[57] Elizabeth Towne died of cardiovascular disease on June 1, 1960. She was remembered in obituaries in the *New York Times* (under the heading "Notables who died this past week"), the *New York Herald Tribune*, and the *World Telegram and Sun*, among others.

ABOUT THE AUTHOR

Tzivia Gover is the author of *Mindful Moments for Stressful Days* (Storey Books, 2002). She received her MFA in Creative Nonfiction from Columbia University and her work has appeared in *The Boston Globe*, *The New York Times*, and *The Christian Science Monitor*, among other publications. She teaches poetry to teen mothers at The Care Center, which is located in Elizabeth Towne's former home in Holyoke, Massachusetts. She is still learning from her students, and from Mrs. Towne, whose spirit continues to infuse the classrooms at The Care Center. The ninth volume of *Nautilus II*, the center's poetry journal, was recently published.